ADVANCE PRAISE

"John's captivating storytelling combined with his desire to share the benefits of leveraging the talent-packed, location-independent workforce make him the ideal spokesperson for the Remote Revolution."

—GREG CAPLAN, FOUNDER/CEO, REMOTE YEAR

"Having run businesses with a fully global footprint for the best part of two decades, I had the privilege of observing the Remote Revolution unfold before it became a 'thing.' We have the great privilege of living in a truly flat world today, with the internet connecting us to incredible opportunities—and with great cost saving—at the tip of our fingers. Talent is now truly global. We can safely scout services from the comfort of our armchair. We can all be digital nomads! This book is a great read for anyone wanting to learn more about this powerful trend."

—STEPHEN VASCONCELLOS-SHARPE, CONVENER OF REBOOT THE FUTURE, PUBLISHER OF SALT

"It's about time someone highlighted insights and benefits of harnessing the power of workforce mobility. John's book is a timely contribution in an era when many employers are wondering how to best capitalize on the capacities of a changing talent pool. As an executive utilizing a mobile workforce for more than a decade, I know the future of work is real and know that those who adapt recruitment and retention practices accordingly will outpace those who don't."

—LAURA COTTON, PUBLIC RELATIONS AND IMAGE DEVELOPMENT MAVEN, PEARL STRATEGIES

"As our diverse group of companies expands, we are yearning for upwardly mobile talent to share our vision with and take our business to the next level. Without remote workers and the ability for talented hires to move about our organization, we would not be able to keep up with the demands of our clients and load, John's insight into how to achieve this is invaluable."

—RENE SEEPERSADSINGH, DIRECTOR, THE SINGH'S GROUP

"*In The Remote Revolution, John details how he embedded himself in one of the world's strongest remote communities. His experiences prove that remote working is a strategic weapon for smart companies to innovate. Today's experts are vast and wide and remote working with today's technology allows the optimal information exchange setup for ideation and execution. 'Clustering' in the twenty-first century is not geographical anymore but rapidly becoming virtual.*"

—DR. MICHAEL MEIGHU, PRINCIPAL
CONSULTANT, PARAGON

"*In 2017, an attachment to a location, desk, or country seems a limiting affair for any creative being, especially to the entrepreneurial-minded. The Remote Revolution touches what is my modus operandi. Being location independent and living between the Caribbean, New York, London, and other cities for Sagaboi has opened up unprecedented opportunities, provided access to top talent, and unveiled inspiring and enriching experiences no singular location could offer.*"

—GEOFF K. COOPER, EDITOR, SAGABOI

THE REMOTE REVOLUTION

THE REMOTE REVOLUTION

HOW THE LOCATION-INDEPENDENT WORKFORCE CHANGES THE WAY WE HIRE, CONNECT, AND SUCCEED

JOHN ELSTON

LIONCREST
PUBLISHING

Cover photo: Tyler Duzan

THE REMOTE REVOLUTION

*How the Location-Independent Workforce Changes
the Way We Hire, Connect, and Succeed*

ISBN 978-1-61961-852-7 *Paperback*
      978-1-61961-851-0 *Ebook*

To Mom and Dad

Thank you.

To Courtney and Jake

I love you.

CONTENTS

INTRODUCTION

THE NEW FRONTIER

I understand the Future of Work. Since becoming a member of a tribe of inspired, adventurous remotes, I've seen young people doing the kinds of work companies would die for. These aren't kids with backpacks and no plans; they're smart and talented entrepreneurs, freelancers, scientists, artists, hiring managers, content curators, former nine-to-fivers, and more. They possess precisely the skillsets that companies want and need to get ahead today. They're collaborative and teamwork oriented, living together in environments they can explore and enjoy. They're also passionate and highly engaged—in short, they're *activated* personally and professionally. I was instantly awed at their capacity, and I still am today.

IT'S A REVOLUTION, BABY

The Remote Revolution is a complete transformation in how we think about work and workforce mobility. Embracing location independence can be a strong point of differentiation (POD) for forward-thinking companies that understand work and life are no longer two separate entities. The revolution is about fusing them together. I learned it because I lived it.

On August 25, 2016, I was living in London. That in itself still seems surreal to me. After three months of living and working around the world, I was still catching myself shaking my head in bewilderment almost every day. It happened so fast—selected out of tens of thousands of applicants and given less than fifty-five days to figure out how to live the next twelve months on four continents, in eight countries, and in twelve cities. I uprooted my entire life, squeezed twenty-three kilos of personal belongings into one suitcase and flew to Central Europe. The landlocked country of the Czech Republic would be the place that I first met seventy-one strangers. All of us shared one common bond: we were going to live together, work together, and most importantly, have life-changing experiences during the next 365 days. Our ages ranged from twenty-three to fifty-three, and we were from seventeen different countries.

We had different backgrounds and a wide range of experience, but we had one thing in common: we all had jobs, a requirement for being selected for the Remote Year program. We met one another for orientation at a gothic warehouse in Prague. The building had been rescued by a local start-up, and the energy from our excitement echoed throughout the natural light-filled, four-story, open-ceiling warehouse.

The meet and greet felt like a speed dating, networking orgy. We bounced from person to person, many of us holding a warm plastic glass of cheap champagne while trying to balance another glass containing amazing ceviche prepared by a local catering company. It went something like this:

"Hi, nice to meet you. My name is John, and I own and run a digital agency I started seven years ago. I'm from California."

"Nice to meet you. My name is Stephan. I am a scientist from Amsterdam."

"Hey! My name is Jeremy, I work for IBM, and I am from Minnesota. Nice to meet you."

"Hi! I'm Hope. I'm a lawyer from New Zealand. Nice to meet you!"

"Hello! I'm Dan, and I work for a nonprofit organization in

New York but also do a lot of freelance work as a developer. Nice to meet you!"

Again and again, I met the people with whom I'd sit next to on buses for fifteen hours with no air conditioning, suffer through weeks of intestinal flu, cook delicious meals, create, laugh, cry, and confide in. We would watch beautiful sunsets and equally beautiful sunrises. Pull all-night hack-a-thons. Take side trips on weekends, sometimes exploring several countries without stopping for sleep or food. We were the living epitome of the overused cliché "Work hard, play hard."

The energy that filled the converted warehouse—and the bond that followed—was *amazing*. We took a group picture that day, one I still treasure. I can remember the way the cold concrete bench felt through my jeans. I can smell the rust from the heavy riveted beams, and I remember the excitement pulsating through the space. What I couldn't remember then but will never forget now were the names of the people on my right and my left in the photograph. A year later, I have a lifetime of stories with seventy-one people whom I didn't previously know but now will never forget. They were inspired, and somehow, we knew we were going to be part of the Remote Revolution.

Before being accepted to the Remote Year family, I had done

my research and learned that one of Remote Year's biggest challenges from the inaugural group before us was having remotes fall out and leave during the twelve-month commitment. The majority of them left because they couldn't find work once they started living remotely. I explained in my interview with the selection team that I had spent hundreds of thousands of dollars the last several years hiring talent across the world—very standard for agencies—and I mentioned I could help solve their challenge by offering freelance work to likeminded remotes. I didn't use it as my platform to get selected, but I know it got their attention.

After meeting and learning more about my fellow remotes, I realized they truly were the kinds of people companies were dying to recruit. Engaged. Driven. Skilled. Talented. Part of my strategy for my own digital marketing agency, Yo!Dog, was that I would use my travels as a way to solve the problems that can be associated with hiring remotely. I was committed to finding high-caliber people who could do great work from anywhere, faster and cheaper. And I did. So can you.

KEY CHALLENGES FACING HIRING TODAY

Before we can talk about the Future of Work, though, we need to start by examining the present—and, for many companies, hiring and retaining top talent is a struggle.

Many of the pain points for talent acquisition professionals don't result from a lack of experience or intelligence, but rather from the speed in which change is coming at them. In *The World Is Flat*, author Thomas Friedman echoes the sentiment that the rate of change is much different now than it has been in the past, writing, "Whenever civilization has gone through one of these disruptive, dislocating technical revolutions—like Gutenberg's introduction of the printing press—the whole world has changed in profound ways."[1] Today, this flattening process is happening at hyperspeed, and it's either directly or indirectly touching many more people around the world at once—far more, certainly, than compared to the introduction of the printing press more than five hundred years ago. That's where the Future of Work—the Remote Revolution—comes into play.

Instead of circumventing this issue by embracing innovative hiring models, many businesses turn to old methodologies, like VUCA, in their approach to hiring and training. **The old VUCA—volatility, uncertainty, complexity, and ambiguity**—was a concept introduced by the US Army War College to describe the facets of the multilateral world at the end of the Cold War. The military trained soldiers to perform during continuous

---

1   Friedman, Thomas L. The world is flat: a brief history of the twenty-first century. Bridgewater, NJ: Distributed by Paw Prints/Baker & Taylor, 2009.

situations, reasoning that if soldiers could perform under the harshest conditions, they'd be prepared for anything. Soon after, companies adopted the goose-and-gander mentality, believing that if such training was good for the military, it was good for corporate America. Instead of leveraging the changes caused by *volatility* into a positive, change-inducing turbulence, companies dug in against it, falling further behind the curve. Refusing to acknowledge volatility led to *uncertainty*, turning what could have been opportunities into difficult long-term decisions. The combination of volatility and uncertainty led to immense—and, often, unnecessary—*complexities* in hiring and training practices. And in the end, the *ambiguity* of the VUCA model—the inability to move forward or adapt that led to negative and reactionary changes in talent management—simply does not work for today's workforce.

Today, while the same level of volatility still exists, it's punctuated by opportunity. Like grass shooting up through cracks in the sidewalk in Valencia where I lived and worked, you have to be paying attention, or you might walk right past and never see the growth. Worse yet, you might trip over the fresh ideas—the future—right in front of you in plain sight.

It's time for a new VUCA.

Winning the talent war today takes **VUCA Prime—vision, understanding, clarity, and agility.** VUCA Prime was developed by Bob Johansen from the Institute for the Future and author of *Leaders Make the Future: Ten New Leadership Skills for an Uncertain World.* The premise of VUCA Prime is simple: companies need to have a clear *vision* of how they will differentiate themselves in a marketplace crowded with teams vying for the same top talent. To get ahead, companies must *understand* what the up-and-coming group of workers want and need. Understanding is one thing but taking action is another—that's where *clarity* comes in. Companies must have one foot in the future at all times, remaining *agile* enough not only to survive in the ever-changing talent market but also to thrive in that innovative space.

Besides being agile, companies must also be strong. Accommodating the flexibility desired by the two fresh generations leading and running companies—millennials and Generation Zers—will require change. And change, especially in the corporate world, can be unpopular. Scary, even. Early adopters who break through will need the passion that capable young workers are drawn to. The revised VUCA mindset is an amazing talent magnet, pulling in talent with incredible force; the old VUCA mindset will send those prospects packing.

THE VALUE OF VUCA PRIME

Regardless of industry, companies today largely face the same types of problems: it's difficult to find great talent, reduce turnover, and distinguish themselves from their competitors. Why? Old-school hiring methods don't account for a new-school workforce, and there are many more chances for talented individuals to land paid opportunities doing what they love in ways that have nothing to do with location. The traditional approach to hiring (i.e., bring in the candidate with the most experience, best education, and highest likelihood to stay put) isn't the way to acquire the most effective and engaged team members.

VUCA Prime will always apply because there is volatility everywhere; recently, we've seen this to be true with President Trump in the United States and Brexit in Europe. The concept of cultural, societal, and economic volatility that touches everything, even hiring practices, isn't time-stamped—it's evergreen. If I wrote this book two decades ago or two decades in the future, the same would be true: the needs of the young workforce are changing because of the amplified volatility they face or, better said, they *don't want* to face. It's not a run-and-hide mentality; rather, it's simply because economic factors like higher overall costs of living have less impact on them. They are agile, non-debt loaded, and not nearly as driven by fear as those bogged down with mortgages, families, revolving debt, and jobs that hold expectations of climbing the ranks to survive.

The juxtapositions between the concepts in the old VUCA and VUCA Prime couldn't be clearer or more important. Vision allows hiring managers to work through the volatility, not struggle against it. Understanding permits leaders to listen and deliver the experiences their employees desire. It takes away the sense of uncertainty that accompanies the double-edged sword of trying to navigate an ever-changing marketplace with an ever-changing, dissatisfied team. Clarity allows leaders to see past the complexities that can cloud hiring today, opening doors for growth that wouldn't be there otherwise. Agility enables hiring managers to find solutions and innovate through the plague of ambiguity.

How can companies break free of the old VUCA and leverage VUCA Prime? It starts by looking at hiring differently.

CONVERSATION AND CULTIVATION

The cobbled street in Belgrade, Serbia, bustled with foot traffic as the barista worked, and the predominately local customers held casual conversations in a language I didn't understand. I was amazed how in just thirty-two days of living abroad, my mind was at ease. My constant fight with attention deficit disorder (ADD) was at an all-time low, a fact I attributed largely to my brain not attempting to comprehend multiple conversations happening around me. Serbian, Hungarian, and Romanian are the three primary languages spoken in Belgrade. Despite my attempt to learn at least fifty native words in each country I lived, it was never enough.

Even with the café as busy as it was that afternoon, I sat at a high-top table where I could watch for Justin, a fellow remote. His apartment was roughly one kilometer from the café and on the same block.

• Justin was one of the most professionally experienced and undoubtedly one of the most financially successful remotes in our group. He was a vice-president at Merrill Lynch prior to starting his own wealth management company in 2010. This was a guy who always looked like he just finished a photo shoot for *GQ*—and, of course, who had the epicurean palette to write reviews for *Gastronomica*. He was unsurprisingly easy to spot as he made his way toward me in his bright orange flipped-collar Ralph Lauren polo, perfectly creased white Bermuda shorts, and black Gucci loafers with no socks. How he dressed like he did with such little luggage amazed me.

Justin squeezed in between the makeshift planter that

acted as the boundary marker between the café and the pedestrian street. I was never sure when he and I got together what the topic of conversation would entail. Most of the time, I learned things like trends in the emerging markets or why the Montecristo No. 2 is overrated, and the Partagás Serie D is the best kept secret. That day, though, was different. Meeting Justin that Wednesday afternoon in Belgrade solidified the primary reason I became so passionate about writing this book.

Our watered-down iced coffees arrived just as Justin leaned in with his question.

"John, you have a lot of contacts back in the US," he said. "Maybe you can help me. I need to find a good accounting person with experience in data entry and account reconciliation—oh, and it would be great if they charged less than $25 an hour."

Justin was right; I *did* have many contacts back home, but my thoughts did not go stateside when Justin suggested I might know someone who could help him solve his accounting problems on a budget. If I *had* let my thoughts go there, I couldn't have found anyone in his price range. Instead, my mind went to the incredibly talented people I had met in the countries I had been living. More specifically, it went to my new friends and community that made up my new family of location-independent professionals.

Like most conversations between remotes, the dialogue seamlessly moved from helping Justin solve his business talent needs to what always seemed a more surreal topic: reliving our recent experiences on our shared journey as we lived and worked around the world.

We finished our coffees, sweating in the sun in the middle of the warmest month Belgrade had seen in a decade. We laughed and replayed the thirty-six-hour escapade from the week prior that took Justin and I via rental car from Prague to Bratislava to Vienna and finally Serbia, where we were living and working for the next thirty-three days. Despite the heat, I was comfortable and happy. More than that, I was *inspired* and on a mission to cultivate the Future of Work.

OFFICE NOT REQUIRED

One of the mantras echoed by remote workers is "Office not required." Iconic entrepreneurs and authors Jason Fried and David Heinemeier Hansson teamed up to write their second best seller, *Remote*, in 2013, subtitling their book with that same mantra. Just a short time later, the ideas and protocols of remote work have evolved. First, it was the Friday work-from-home option, then came the four-day workweek, job sharing, and coming into the office once a week for meetings. Finally, a new generation of workers—tens of thousands like me and my team—are committed to being 100 percent remote.

There is a revolutionary leap from working remotely at home and being location independent. It blows my mind how many respected companies allow a good percentage of their employees to do varying degrees of remote work, yet they insist that remote means working from a converted guest bedroom or closet in their home. That view is shortsighted and false.

To me, being remote means working from your Airbnb in cities and countries like Córdoba, Argentina, on a gig team—a collection of talented, driven, fellow remotes—having blazing-fast Wi-Fi, freelancing as a solo specialist, or working for one of the world's forward-thinking companies and using collaboration tools like Zoom, Slack, WhatsApp, or any of the dozens of other affordable tools accessible all over the world.

I'll tell you a secret: I almost titled this book *Remotely Inspired*. Friends and my publisher, though, were afraid my readers might misconstrue that title. After all, "remotely" can also mean "to the slightest degree"—a definition that is the opposite of my experience as a remote. To me, as a living, working remote professional, that title encompassed my truth: I am remotely inspired. I'm inspired at a level I have never been before *because* I am remote. Regardless of your industry or your job title, we can all agree that we are happiest and do our best work when we are truly inspired, as I am. So why aren't more companies leading the way, capturing the flag, and winning the talent war by having the most inspired workforce in the world?

Throughout the book, I hope to answer that question—and continue the Remote Revolution—through accomplishing two primary goals.

1. **Tell relatable, true, and genuine stories of my experiences as a remote, so you can understand the level of inspiration, exhilaration, camaraderie, and dedication remote professionals feel.** But, most importantly, explain how the experiences and lifestyle empower some of the best talent in the world to a higher level of company loyalty and appreciation that leads them to doing the best work of their lives. You don't have to hike the Inca Trail, make the trek to the top of Machu Picchu, or take a forty-eight-hour weekend side trip to Cartagena to harness the power of this inspiration. Instead, you just have to be able to wrap your mind around one fact: as an HR policy

maker, CEO, entrepreneur, or hiring manager, that talent you're searching for is out there. They are ready to work hard and make sacrifices for the betterment of the companies they want to work for—or, in many cases, the freelance gigs you contract them for. They choose to be remote because they *look at life differently*. And to win the talent war, so should you. It's time to let go of old-school hiring regiments and policies that confine and restrict your access to and chances of attracting the talent that put gas in the engine of the Future of Work.

2. **Provide firsthand knowledge of what qualities to look for in remote professionals.** It's obvious, but I'm going to say it anyway: just because an individual is a remote with skills to live around the world doesn't mean they are guaranteed to be an amazing employee. As a business owner, I'm acutely aware of this fact—and I'll share my experiences of successfully navigating the ups and downs of hiring and managing remote professionals. I will offer insights on building a network of the world's best talent. I hope that by sharing this level of detail, it will improve your success, lessen your perceived risk, and ultimately give your company a POD among your competitors.

EXPERIENCE IS THE REWARD

Back in Belgrade, Justin and I finished sweating through our afternoon coffees. We headed off in different directions but agreed to meet up in a couple of days after I had given some thought to helping him solve his accounting talent need.

I walked back to the remote office, where I bumped into Milan. Milan, a twenty-six-year-old born in Belgrade, had been hired by Remote Year to be a city manager. The primary job of a city manager was to act as a direct resource for our remote community and provide an array of services. In short, Milan was tasked with being the perfect combination of a concierge and local advocate for all seventy-two of us. He had taken the job for unobvious reasons. One would think that the primary motive to take such a demanding and unpredictable position with a still-to-be-proven-start-up would have been to supplement his income. After all, new jobs are very hard to come by in a country that, in recent years, has seen unemployment rates rise as high as 42 percent in the Belgrade region.

But Milan had different reasons. He had done his homework and knew that hundreds of thousands of talented professionals were applying for only a few golden tickets—not the kind that get you a private tour of a chocolate factory, but the kind that would hand deliver writers, programmers, designers, investors, sales professionals, and creatives to his front door—people with contacts, vision, and proven track records for executing on good ideas. The very people Milan would be shuttling around, making dinner reservations for, and providing maps and ideas for side trips would provide him with more opportunities and exposure to pitch his own ideas and business plans than most get from being an alumnus at a private college.

That day, he stopped me outside our workspace and offered a proposition. "I'd like to take you to dinner tonight and pitch a couple of ideas I have," he said. It was nothing new for me to entertain the request, as I'd often been both privy to and part of detailed pitches, presentations, and disruptive idea brainstorming sessions in my daily life and business. So, just barely into my second month aboard, I quickly agreed.

That evening, Milan pitched two great business plans. One that resonated with me focused on the talent and manpower-resourcing field. Over the next several days, Milan set up meetings and interviews for me to connect with talented people in his network. I was blown away by the quality and excitement of everybody I met.

Within twenty-four hours of sitting in the café with Justin, I was introducing him to amazing fresh talent with affordable expectations. Justin hired a woman on the spot who had a college degree and accounting experience. After Justin hired her, Milan and I continued to brainstorm about teams of talent, teams that we later called garage teams, because they often worked remotely in low-rent apartments or garages.[2]

Eventually, I hired a phenomenal garage team from Milan's network to do work for my company. I had always hired contract employees and freelancers from around the world for projects both short- and long term, but those earlier efforts lacked the connection and level of communication I wish I had. Those individuals were more task oriented and not part of a team.

This time, though, I was far more successful. Why? For starters, I was a remote, and they were a local remote team. We understood more clearly what needed to be accomplished, and I also could use Milan as the acting project manager to bridge any communication gaps and provide local oversight. Still months after I moved to other parts of the world, it was a very manageable and profitable situation.

---

2   Garage teams (or gig teams) are small, experienced groups of individuals who have special individualized skills and work together as a collective. Often, they've previously worked together and have concluded that joining forces not only allows them to provide tremendous value and results professionally, but that working together also gives them a level of personal satisfaction and opportunity above anything they'd be able to achieve working for a large company.

BEYOND THE BORDER

I felt a sense of accomplishment in reducing pain points for Justin and my own company, and I wanted to reward myself with a weekend side trip and go exploring. As a remote, you seize every opportunity to take advantage of where you live. By design, we always transitioned our moves to other cities and countries on weekends. The good news for employers, clients, and our own enterprises was we never took time away from what is traditionally known as the standard workweek. Weekends were for moving or exploring. That particular weekend, I opted for the latter.

After our meeting, I mentioned to Milan that I was looking for something to do that weekend. As a remote, I'd decided my mantra for this season of my life would be different than the three decades of my past professional life: Don't oversteer. Instead, accept that it is OK to let opportunities unfold without detailed planning or, more importantly, don't commit to making things happen as much as letting them happen. Later, this became a critical part of my success as a remote living and working around the world. When Milan suggested I visit the Uvac Special Nature Reserve that shares its borders with Serbia and Bosnia to see the majestic griffon vulture, I was sold.

When the weekend came, my roommate Tyler and I

hopped into a rented Fiat Punto—a compact and not-so-mighty vehicle that manufacturers claim could top out at ninety-five miles per hour but that really reached a maximum of around fifty-three miles per hour on a good day—and headed west. We had no road map or Google map. After a wrong turn, our four-hour drive turned into an eleven-hour adventure. We finally made it to the town of Sjenica. We ate at a quaint street-side café in the small town known primarily for its cultural heritage, sheep, and cheese. As I scanned through my iPhone trying to plan our moves for the next day, Tyler struck up a conversation with two men at an adjacent table, whom I'd come to know as Emir and his cousin. Tyler, who took more time and pride than I did in learning words and phrases from the native languages of the countries in which we lived, solidified our newfound relationship with our two new Serbian and Bosnian friends by mispronouncing several Serbian words. In fact, he proposed marriage to one of them rather than expressing gratitude for their input on tactics we should use in our adventure scheduled for the next morning. After some awkward laughter, Emir cleared things up by speaking perfectly clear English. He told Tyler he would have to decline the proposal, but he had a better idea.

"We'll take you to see the amazing birds, and I will also arrange for both of you to meet my friend and his family. He will take you on his boat to see many amazing things,"

Emir said. "This is our country, and we'd love to share it with you. We have a truck, and we know right where to take you." They didn't ask us to pay a fee. We didn't purchase any tickets. Immediately, we just agreed to meet early the next morning. I felt safe. Comfortable. Like I'd found two new friends in a country that no longer felt as foreign.

The next day, the four of us met early for breakfast, and then we drove about forty-five minutes to Sjenica Lake before getting into a four-passenger aluminum boat with Emir, his cousin, and our 475-pound shirtless boat captain and headed out onto the Uvac River. We arrived at Ledena Cave, also known as Cold Cave. The caves lay at the base of Uvac Canyon. While not a Serbian secret, it was a surprise to me to be experiencing one of the most beautiful natural sites I have ever seen. We reveled in the etchings embedded in the cave walls made by hundreds of years of flowing water.

From there, Emir guided us further. We hiked several miles of rigorous plateaued shelves and hills covered in lush vegetation. We arrived at our destination—a wooden hand-carved perch no less than 450 meters off the ground suspended over the cliff. I stepped over the tree branches carved into a makeshift fence and sat on a rock on the other side of the barrier, my feet dangling over the drop-off. The stillness of the moment was captured by Tyler and his Nikon. That image of me on that inspiring day is the cover photo of this book.

Below me, the Uvac River glistened in the sun, emerald, pristine, and untouched by boats. I was both exhilarated and awed, both content and inspired. It hit me then: I didn't need to see a griffon vulture. There with Tyler and my two new Serbian and Bosnian friends, I realized it was the experience itself that made me feel so alive, not the expected result of seeing large birds. It was more than enough.

We didn't see any vultures that day, but we headed back the next day to try again. In the same place, at the same time of day, we saw dozens of once almost-extinct griffon vultures floating majestically right in front of us, their wingspans between seven and ten feet wide. As I stood in Uvac National Reserve—the largest protected nesting ground for the griffon vulture—I was in blown awayof the sheer size and graze of the birds. Simply being in their presence was breathtaking.

I have had motivational experiences like this one in every country I've lived in while traveling as a remote. Sometimes they were subtle; other times they were as grand as the wingspan of a griffon vulture. Every time, though, they have inspired me, allowing me to bring a new level of productivity and enthusiasm to my work. Again, it made me realize that working for reward is worth every second.

In these moments, I've often wished other leaders and executives could see what I've seen, felt what I've felt. I know they're searching for the missing piece that will solve their talent problems and help them set their businesses apart—challenges I remember all too well, because I lived them. Bottom line: I've been fortunate enough to have a front seat to the Future of Work, and I'm here to share it.

A NEW PERSPECTIVE ON HIRING

If you couldn't already tell, this isn't your typical book on hiring.

You've read books about how to attract and retain the best employees. You've read books about how to source talent for start-ups, and how to run margin analysis to determine the correct head counts. You've read books about what's working and what isn't when it comes to the people aspect of business. You've read books by people who work remotely in between travels, moving from place to place, and recounting their adventures.

This is none of those books. And it's all those books.

How? Because collectively throughout my life, I have lived in the role of employee, manager, business owner, entrepreneur, and now remote. I am in the position to approach the topic of traveling remote workers from each of those perspectives. I grew my career in the corporate world. I've spent thirty years starting and running numerous businesses. Then, in 2015, I decentralized my marketing agency and opted to work while living in the world for a year. In the pages of this book, I want to share what I have been so fortunate to learn. I'm going to tell you why and how important it is to be a part of the Remote Revolution.

The following chapters take a deep dive into the remote movement—that is, the increasing number of talented workers who choose to be location independent, allowing them to work and live inspired. In my book, I'll examine all the facets of the movement and answer all your burning questions (like the following):

How did this revolution come to fruition?

What *is* this revolution? Is it something that can scale and be sustained?

How do you jump into the revolution and win the talent war?

What does creating and implementing a global policy on remote work *look* like?

No, I did not set out on my remote journey intending to write a book, but it gradually occurred to me while living around the world that this book needed to be written. Now, at fifty-four years old, it's true that I am an unlikely spokesperson for the remote movement, but I've been a part of all sides of it. It has changed the way I live and, most importantly, it has taught me to look at life differently.

PERSONAL CONNECTIONS

As much as I wanted to get to know everybody in our remote family, I was realistic. As I set off for my year of living and working around the world, I did not have expectations to deeply connect with each of the seventy-one other remotes. I knew it would have been impossible to enjoy and learn from every one of them. I also knew that just because we all shared the common bond of being selected to join Remote Year, I wouldn't be compatible with everybody in the group—and vice versa. However, I also did not expect several of the remotes to impact my life—both personally and professionally—as strongly as they did. Throughout this book, I am going to share details and stories about these amazing people who came into my life. Why? It's simple: the purpose of this book is to amplify the message that unbelievable talent—talent with high capacities for work, creative minds, and dedication to their jobs—can be loyal employees working from anywhere in the world. Oh, and by the way, people with those attributes also make incredible friends.

I met Dhivyakrishnan on May 30, 2016, officially my second day as an international remote. Dhivya (pronounced Div-ēa) was born in the town of Kovilpatti, in the state of Tamil Nadu in the southernmost part of the Indian Peninsula. Dhivya, an automation software engineer, is a dual citizen. She gets her mail delivered to Seattle, Washington, but she lives around the world. She's in no way homeless—Dhivya, like me, is *home-free*.

The Prague air was crisp and cold that morning, and the combination of hot steam from my double espresso to-go and the small cloud of air from my breathing were racing each other backward against my morning uphill walk home. My brisk walk back to my apartment took me past the Katedrála Svateho Vita (Cathedral of Saints Vitus, Wenceslaus, and Adalbert). The cathedral was dedicated only to Saint Vitus and is still commonly named only as Saint Vitus Cathedral. It is an incredible example of

Gothic architecture and is the largest most important church in the country.

As I approached the exterior door to my apartment building and attempted to balance my coffee and backpack in one hand, I fumbled to find my keys. Standing outside her apartment immediately next door was Dhivya and several other remotes. As good as I am with being chivalrous, I am horrible with remembering names and pronunciation. After a couple months of mumbling her name incorrectly, I just shortened it to Dhivya.

Dhivya would go on to become one of my very good friends and roommates, with a passion for travel matched only by her passion for life and her professional expertise. At thirty-three years old, she has wander lusted around the world living in more than one hundred countries, a feat that is achieved by fewer than .001 percent of the human population. This accomplishment stretches my mind when I reflect on the fact that she has only been living on this earth for barely three decades. You see, Dhivya is not financially wealthy. She is not supported by a family trust. Dhivya is an automation software engineer—a very good one. She never misses a deadline, and she organizes and manages a team from halfway around the world. Dhivya was promoted twice and offered a third promotion in the short time I've known her. But her life is not magic, and her job is not perfect. It's hard work every day and every night, but in the true outstanding employee fashion, she puts her work first. Her company respects her and knows they have one of the most inspired, talented engineers in the world. Dhivyakrishnan is not the exception to the Remote Revolution—she is the potential talent that exists.

BETTER TOGETHER

Often, location-independent workers will find one another before they are tasked to work together. They find commonalities tied to interests that originate outside of work. Activities like hiking, running, videography, cooking, and, of course, exploring the foundation for future accomplishments socially and professionally. These bonds built during non-pressure qualitative time together prepare the team for future high-pressure professional success.

In traditional work relationships, getting together and cooking a communal dinner or going for a morning run are most often by-products or conclusions to spending abhorrent amounts of time together in nonsocial, high-pressure work environments. When the origin of team building lies in complex environments that include conflict, deadlines, and other circumstances that cause stress, it's harder to perform at exceptional levels as a team. However, when a group gets together professionally after first spending time together socially, the results can be phenomenal—an event I witnessed time and time again during my experience. Some of the best teamwork and creativity I have ever seen came after a group of remotes spent time together socially for months before coming together to launch business and philanthropic platforms that became successful. I watched from the outside-in as a group of remote friends launched a collaborative idea they called the Valencia Project, a vibrant social network that connects creatives from around the world and gives them an opportunity to promote their creative content. The creators of the Valencia Project all had their own skillsets and wanted to come together as a team to create an opportunity for other creatives around the world, so they divided the necessary duties and launched the successful platform. You can read more about their work at www.johnelston.com.

If I would have tried to launch the Valencia Project as a traditional start-up, it would have taken months to identify the right talent, required a significant amount of capital, and been accompanied by a high risk of failure. At the end of the day, the reality is too many great ideas never make it off the drawing board, and if they do, the chances of these businesses succeeding is so low that they usually crash and burn.

Instead of working in the pressure cooker of building an entire team one player at a time, it's more efficient to find a team that has put themselves together. Next time you're considering hiring a handful of independent experts for a project, consider consolidating your postings. Instead of three or four openings, post one description that requires applicants to apply as a team. Use remote-driven sites like flexjobs.com and keywords like "gig team" and "remote team." You'll be blown away by the talent and experience of teams ready to knock the ball out of the park.

On one of my travels, I saw a gig team working in a coffee shop. They were laughing, collaborating, and buying one another espresso shots. Their energy was contagious. After a few hours of hard-core collaborating, they all got up and went out to explore together. Their dynamic was so effortless and energetic that it gave me goose bumps. They, and so many others like them, are proof that employers no longer have to feel obligated to have employee recognition events, hold holiday parties, or hand out awards. For the next generation of creatives, *experiences is the reward.* That's why they can charge fair prices for the same, if not better, work—because their perk is their freedom, and that's invaluable.

But wait, am I *really* suggesting you should not expect your employees to come into work every day? You bet—here's why.

WHY YOU SHOULDN'T EXPECT PEOPLE TO COME INTO WORK EVERY DAY

It seems reasonable to expect your employees to come into work every day—or does it?

Part of the faux appeal of a traditional office setup can be explained by what's called the skyscraper theory—that is, a company has success, then banks on building the largest, fanciest office space to attract and retain top performers. For example, they could brag about having the biggest building in San Francisco—a billion-dollar investment in one of the world's most expensive cities—never realizing they could get the same (or likely better) talent without the hit on their bottom line.

I understand it's obviously possible to succeed without embracing location independence, but how long will that last? When a company embraces remote work and starts attracting capable, inspired young people who call themselves remotes, they'll start attracting better talent immediately. No wait. They can focus on building a business instead of building a skyscraper to hold it.

YES AND NO

Often, I'm asked if hiring garage teams from around the world takes jobs away from teams in the United States.

My answer? Yes and no. Yes, hiring a team like the one in Belgrade did mean I didn't hire one in the States. However, by peeling back the skin of the hiring onion, you'll see the "no." Working with the Belgrade team allowed me to offer a deliverable to a new sector of small businesses back in the United States that could otherwise not afford my services. We were then able to build complete online presences for a slew of small US-based businesses. Remember, the largest and still fastest-growing population of location-independent professionals hail from the United States, a figure specifically true of my new remote family. Although we represented seventeen countries, there were significantly more remotes from the United States than any other place in the world. As an embedded CEO of my own company, I could offer opportunities to US citizens who were part of our community dozens of times throughout the year.

THE FUTURE IS NOW

Working remotely for the past year and traveling the world has been inspiring. Not only are my fellow remotes and I living our dreams, but we're also much more productive and engaged with our work. The life of the traveling remote worker gives me the most balance. And of course, it does! It seems like a no-brainer, right? The setup is good for individuals because it gives them flexibility and freedom. It's also good for employers because it provides cost-effective solutions and happier employees. Last but certainly not least, it's good for the world because communities across the globe benefit from the philanthropic and volunteer activities many traveling remote workers participate in during their free time.

Why *wouldn't* businesses want to move in this direction? Here's a secret: some of them do. From my unique vantage point, it's clear to me that the rise of the traveling remote worker isn't the "future" of work at all—it's happening now. Savvy companies are already shifting their focus to source short-term talent and hire gig teams, getting the best teams for the best prices. They're reconfiguring the talent supply chain from the bottom up. They're embracing the new VUCA, and they're getting results.

But not every company is so quick to get on board.

CONVINCING THE HATERS

Part of any revolution is disruption of the norm, and departures from "business as usual" can be worrisome, especially when the profitability and sustainability of your entire company is on the line. The rise of location-independent gigonomists—that is, remotes—threatens traditional hiring practices that have existed for decades.

I understand that.

As a decision maker, you likely thrive on data when it comes to contemplating shifts in your business; you want case studies and historical proof. You want to run the numbers. Because we're just on the cusp of the Remote Revolution, that data isn't available yet, and that's scary.

I understand that.

There's an unwritten rule among HR hiring managers that most of the best people are already working for someone else. Even though you may secretly *know* you're losing the talent war, you might look at location independence as self-serving and rooted too heavily in self-promotion over company betterment.

I understand that.

Companies that are managing to attract and retain top talent using old-school methods may scoff at the notion of embracing a new kind of hiring paradigm. If it isn't broken, why throw a wrench in things and try to fix it anyway? What's the benefit? It feels unclear.

I understand that, too.

I also understand that despite all those hesitations, the rise of location-independent workers and gig teams *is* the Future of Work. There is no doubt in my mind. Although I've lived both sides of it, the revolution is new to me, too, and still sometimes feels a little strange. I know I'd rather position my business ahead of the curve, though, remaining proactive instead of reactive to the changing talent market.

Bottom line: Many businesses are still in denial and fully unprepared to deal with the Remote Revolution—and I *get* it. Maybe you're in the process of building a three-block-long office in downtown San Francisco. Maybe you've spent hundreds of millions of dollars on corporate training programs and incentivizing local employees. You don't want to hear that the future isn't in some office space—at least not your office space.

Part of the creative energy that feeds remotes is flexibility, a change of scenery, and a high-performance workspace. I think there are several stigmas attached to the remote worker, one of which is they do most of their work secluded from the world and never know if they are going to have good cell coverage or great Wi-Fi. This assumption is not even close to being true. Most get up every day, make their bed, and exercise or meditate. They journal, review the week's task list, and then walk to work.

What? Wait. Walk to work? Yes, that's right. I walked to work almost every day in Prague, Belgrade, Valencia, Lisbon, and Rabat, just to name a few. In some cities, the round-trip walk was three blocks, and in others, it was three miles. Incredible co-working space is at the fingertips of anyone who wants to walk through the doors and get to work. Most communal workspaces allow day passes, week- or month-long terms—or, in some cases, even a permanent desk with your name on it.

Personally, I am a huge fan and member of WeWork, a genius start-up cofounded by Adam Neumann and Miguel McKelvey. I discovered WeWork while living in Europe. Since the day I walked into my first WeWork office a year ago, I have become a one-man crusade telling anyone who would listen and taking anyone who will go with me to WeWork spaces all over the world, from Orange County, California, to the twenty-third floor of the recently launched WeWork in Buenos Aires, Argentina.

To varying degrees, we all have an intuitive radar about things that are going to be a runaway hit. The first time you hear a brilliant song on the radio or eat a delicious sandwich from the new deli around the corner, you can tell they have something different—and that something is amazing. *That* is exactly how I felt about WeWork. Now that I live and work around the world without the support of Remote Year, I plan my own destinations and accommodations. I have been known to start the process of discovery by first checking to see if there is a WeWork space in the city I am considering. (Learn more about WeWork at www.johnelston.com.)

Writers and authors strive to present their readers with relative and trending content. The speed to market of a blog post or print article, then, is obviously easier than writing content for a book that may not be available for months—sometimes years—after the words have been written. This book in your hands has been rattling around in my head for more than a year, and it finally started to make its way to paper about nine months ago. I committed to my publisher and my editor that I would lock my manuscript—stop fiddling with it and put it into their skilled hands to polish and bring to life—on Friday, October 13, 2017. That was the plan until 10:00 p.m. the night before my deadline when I got off a plane in Chicago and passed a gift shop on my way to connect to my next flight. My eyes were drawn to the gift shop window, and strategically placed at eye level along the entire length of the window were thirty-five horizontally aligned copies of the October 2017 edition of *Forbes*. The face on the cover stopped me in my tracks. It was a confident headshot of Adam Neumann. Instead of fumbling for my glasses, I pressed my nose up against the window to read the small-font quote under Adam's name set on the left side of the cover: "WE'RE DOING AMAZING THINGS THAT NO ONE ELSE IS DOING." Then, I gazed at the featured article's title, centered, in a large-size font.

THE $20 BILLION OFFICE PARTY

I didn't know what to do. I didn't know how to feel.

Less than twenty-four hours before I was supposed to deliver my locked manuscript to my publisher, I wanted to write about the importance of communal workspace. I wanted to share with my readers what *I* already knew but chose to leave out of the book in fear that I would not provide trending content. I felt like the timing of the article was a sign that either my book was coming out too late, or, maybe, it was getting published at just the right time. The optimist that resides inside of me chose the latter, but I still wasn't convinced that my book wouldn't be behind the times before anyone read a word.

I grabbed my phone and called my editor, Jessica. Soft spoken but deliberate, she doesn't waste many words. When I pose one-hundred-mile-per-hour fastball questions and occasional curveballs, they're almost always met with brief silence. I often catch myself saying, "Are you there?" Five or six seconds can seem like an eternity when there is dead air. Then, she responds, and her words are calm and unhurried.

Although it was now almost 11:00 p.m. her time, she answered on the second ring. Our conversation went something like this:

Me: Jess, it's John. You won't believe who and what is on the cover of *Forbes* magazine!

Jess: What? Where are you?

Me: I am standing in front of the Hudson Bookstore in the Chicago airport. Adam Neumann, the cofounder of WeWork, is on the cover.

Jess: OK.

Silence.

Me: Do you think this is a good thing or a bad thing?

Jess: Well, tell me why you think it could be a bad thing.

With just one sentence from her, I feel as though I could

be sitting in therapy. My mind slows down, and I start to talk through the pros and the cons with her.

Jess: If you think sharing the specifics of the WeWork platform is vital to your audience, do it. Don't lock the manuscript tomorrow. It's your book, and we want you to be happy with it.

Me: OK.

Jess: But get it done. Oh, and one other thing: you have to call Kathleen.

(Kathleen, my publisher, is brilliant and helpful. She holds the keys to the asylum and knows that handing them over to the crazy people like me will just slow things down.)

Me: OK, thank you, Jess. Good night.

POD PROOF

If you are reading this, you know I received 100 percent support from my team to delay the lock and add the *Forbes* cover story written by Steven Bertoni,[3] "WeWork's $20

---

3   Steven Bertoni, "WeWork's $20 Billion Office Party: The Crazy Bet That Could Change How the World Does Business," *Forbes*, October 2, 2017, https://www. forbes.com/sites/stevenbertoni/2017/10/02/the-way-we-work/#6ff53afe1b18.

Billion Office Party: The Crazy Bet That Could Change How the World Does Business."

The recent article more than proves that in the race to carve out a POD for your business by securing the best talent, being one of the first ones out of the starting block means thinking outside the handbook. Even more than that, thinking outside the office—literally.

In short, thinking like a remote.

CHAPTER 1

AN UNLIKELY CHAMPION FOR THIS MOVEMENT

I began my experience as one of seventy-two location-independent professionals. The average age? Thirty-one. The youngest—Eddie, an incredibly talented remote who blew me away again and again with his old soul demeanor and his creative prowess—was twenty-three when we started our journey abroad together. The oldest? You guessed it: me. John Elston.

Professionally, we all were the top echelon of our companies or start-ups, exceptionally skilled at communication, organization, and collaboration. We were also a group of self-starters, motivated by community, culture, and cause.

Employers today want employees who embody *all* those traits, yet they go about it the wrong way. I know because I *was* that employer. When it comes to the validity of the Remote Revolution, it's likely the old me wouldn't have been so quick to see the light.

A HISTORY OF TRIGGERS

When I was six years old, I cut out squares of brown butcher paper and glued them to the outside of my lunch box. As I walked to school, I imagined it was a briefcase and that I was headed to a meeting. Rather than documents, it held a cheese sandwich and chips, but I pretended. And pretended. And pretended. I never told my classmates or my parents why I glued the butcher paper to my beat-up lunch box, but *I* knew—I wanted to be just like my dad. It didn't matter that he never carried a briefcase. It mattered that he worked, and I wanted to do the same. Even more, I liked the way it felt, walking proudly with my "briefcase." Purposeful. Important. The mantra of "Work for reward" was embedded into my life starting at a young age. I didn't refer to it as that—and I certainly didn't have it tattooed on the inside of my right bicep like I do now—but I knew that society rewarded you for working hard, and I knew I wanted to be successful.

I put on a tuxedo for the first time a year later as the ring bearer in my aunt's wedding. To this day, I don't remember being in the wedding on that Thursday evening in 1970, but I remember the feeling of the long black tie and shiny shoes. I felt like the successful businessperson I was driven to become, and—again—it suited me. I didn't take the tuxedo off for four days. My mother finally had to slip it off me after I fell asleep.

When I was eleven, I got my first job as a paperboy delivering the *Daily Report* in my small city of Ontario, California. My best friend and next-door neighbor worked there, and I'd taken over his route for him while he went on vacation shortly before being granted my own route. I took being a paperboy exactly as you would expect from a kid who once schlepped glue over his tin lunch box to make a briefcase and had to be physically removed from his first-ever tux: seriously. I wanted to be the best damn paperboy that city had ever seen.

Besides delivering papers to subscribers, part of my job was also to grow the number of subscriptions. Once, the company offered an incentive trip to whomever could sell the most subscriptions in a ten-day period. On day one and for the next nine, I started knocking on doors shortly after sunrise, asking nonsubscribers if they'd like to receive the newspaper for a mere $2.85 per month. Before sunset on the tenth day, I'd sold more subscriptions than anyone on my team.

That year, the highest-selling paperboys and papergirls from Southern California got to take an all-expense-paid trip to San Diego with our managers, spending the weekend at the zoo and theme parks. The incentive trip deepened my desire to excel in business because I wasn't just pretending I was successful anymore; I was experiencing what success felt like. I was hooked. Looking back, I can see those events in my youth—the lunch box, the tuxedo, the incentive trip—as a series of triggers that spurred my intense desire to excel in business.

On a podcast I recently listened to, one of my mentors, Tim Ferriss, gave the following advice about how to find out where you'd excel professionally. Do whatever it is you'd do for free and become great at it, and you'll eventually get paid for it—or, do whatever you were doing when you were eleven years old. In my case, Tim could not have been more spot-on. At eleven, I was selling, working hard, and making people happy. They were especially happy because I learned how to "porch" their daily papers; in other words, I learned how to throw the tightly rubber-band-bound newspaper from the sidewalk such that it would land precisely on my customer's porch—all while pedaling as fast as I could on my bike. When I wasn't satisfying current customers, I was selling new customers on the benefits of subscribing to the paper.

WE ALL COULD LEARN SOMETHING
FROM THE HOSPITALITY INDUSTRY

At eighteen, I interviewed and was hired in an industry that unbeknown to me would be a perfect fit—so perfect I would spend the next thirty-two years of my life mastering the art and business of hospitality. As a bellman, I had typical guest service responsibilities—driving the courtesy van to and from the airport, carrying bags, and so forth. I didn't have any formal training and I wasn't even aware that I was good at it. What I *did* recognize was that the more I worked, the more money I made. Day in, day out, I made more tips than every bellman in the hotel. Some days, I actually made more money than the *collective* group of bellmen working that day.

We all had the same opportunities, and we all wore the same tan-and-brown polyester-blend monkey suits, but there was one major POD. (I had created my first POD!) None of the other bellmen wanted to be away from the phone when the guests called down to have their luggage picked up. The standard tip for retrieving a cart full of bags from a guestroom was five dollars. Occasionally, you could make ten dollars. Delivering an iron and ironing board or a hair dryer was NEVER more than a one-dollar tip. (Yes, irons, boards, and blow dryers had to be delivered to rooms upon request.) A fifteen-minute round trip to the airport averaged a three-dollar tip.

I quickly discovered I could deliver irons and boards and an occasional blow dryer before a single call would come in to pick up a load of luggage. I took my POD to the next level by asking guests when I delivered their requested item if they had a desired time they would like me to come back and get their luggage. Not only did I get the tip for the delivery, but I would also show up at the guests' door with the luggage cart—all without their ever having to pick up the phone. At the end of my eight-hour shift, my pockets were stuffed with dollar bills and mixed with an occasional five-dollar bill.

My POD flew under the radar of management until the day I went to the human resources office and requested an additional bellman's coat. The HR director looked at me like I had two heads and asked, "Why on earth do you want a second coat?" Little did I know my response would catapult my career from bellman to boss!

I explained to the puzzled executive committee member that I needed the second coat to wear when I drove the van to the airport. I told her I was so sweaty every day from running the halls delivering irons and boards that guests would roll down the windows in the van to let in fresh air. I told her with a second coat, I could switch coats in the bellman's closet before I jumped in the van. Her dumbfounded gaze turned into a piercing, squinted-eye stare. She didn't say a word. She got up from her desk, went into the uniform room, and retrieved a coat. I signed the bright pink form she handed me without a thought and quickly ran to the bellman's closet, readying the coat for my next trip to the airport.

The next day, I showed up for my shift, and my buddy Jim, another bellman, said, "Dude, Mr. Sannes called and said you need to go to his office the second you get in." I didn't know what that meant, but it felt like I was getting called into the principal's office. I had worked at the hotel for only about a month and had not even met Mr. Sannes, much less been summoned to his office. Dennis Sannes was the general manager (GM) of the hotel; in the hospitality business, he was the equivalent to the mayor of a city or a general in the army.

I stepped into Mr. Sannes's office, an office so large that I didn't even see the HR director sitting on the sofa fifteen yards to my left. Mr. Sannes motioned me to sit down in one of the two overstuffed ruby red paisley-patterned chairs. He didn't say a word for what seemed like the length of time that I could have made two ironing board runs, but in reality, it was probably more like fifteen seconds. Looking at me (but talking to the HR director), he said in a gruff, raspy-throated voice, "He doesn't look sweaty to me." It was then that I realized he was talking to the person responsible for offering me the job just a month ago.

The top of Mr. Sannes's desk was spotless. No business cards. No stapler. Not even a pen or pencil. Then I saw it—I caught a glimpse of the bright pink form I'd signed earlier positioned under his right forearm. I watched as he pulled the skin on his neck below his double chin, and then he picked up the form with his right hand. *I'm going to get fired from my first real job*, I thought. Then, looking right into my eyes, he said, "Explain to me why you needed a second bell coat."

I swallowed hard and gave the same explanation I did the day before in the HR office. Again, silence from the stoic veteran hotelier. Finally, he asked, "How much money do you make in tips every day, Jim?" I must have looked like I was going to puke on the top of his clean desk. "What's wrong with you?" he asked.

"My name is John, sir," I said. I could see his face turning as red as the chair I was sitting in.

"Then why are you wearing a name tag that says Jim?" he bellowed. I had forgotten my name tag at home, and my bellman buddy, Jim, suggested I wear his name tag to my believed firing. Without hesitation and acting as though I hadn't heard his prior question, I responded, "Sixty-five dollars a day on average, sir."

"How do you feel about taking a pay cut?" he asked. *Sure, that's better than getting fired*, I thought. I nodded quickly in the affirmative.

"Good, we'd like to put you in our management training program. Now go back to work, and for God's sake, put on the right name tag," he said.

Four years later, at age twenty-two, I was running a 250-room hotel in Spokane, Washington, that generated more than six million dollars in revenue annually.

CHASING SUCCESS

My meeting with Mr. Sannes was more than thirty-six years ago, but the lessons I took from that experience and all those before it are more relevant than ever. Most remotes want to work hard and are constantly looking for ways to create their own PODs. They are willing to perform smaller jobs for less money like I was willing to do three decades before them, running irons and boards. Why? In the end, they know there will be a Mr. Sannes who recognizes they are disruptive and are doing things differently than others with their same skillsets.

For decades, it was the same dynamic: employers were looking for human capital, trying to attract the best talent. Employees bought into the idea of the collective definition of professional growth—accumulate wealth, put down roots, climb the corporate ladder. And I was one of them. I'd fallen in love with business. Not only that, but I was good at it. I felt validated. I had subscribed to the "work for reward" model my entire life; it was my reality, and I was creating it.

That's why, just a few credits shy of completing my college degree in psychology, I quit. I dropped out of school. I had a partial football scholarship but had gotten injured and was taking eighteen to twenty credits per semester while working two jobs, one as a bellman and one in a home for adults with disabilities (in accordance with my degree path). Never an exceptional student in the first place, I got burned out. After Mr. Sannes put me in the management training program, I quickly went from being a bellman to a front desk supervisor to a coffee shop/restaurant supervisor. Then, the opportunity choice became real—I could continue down the management line, but I'd need to move to the corporate hotel in Sacramento, California, to do it. I did just that.

I rented a truck, filled it with everything I owned, and moved out of my parents' house. I never looked back. My parents supported me a million percent, a fact that helped immensely. One year after I signed that pink slip for a second uniform, My career was in motion. I got married and that same year began the management training program. The program was fast-paced; even when I wasn't on the clock, I was working in other departments of the hotel, trying to learn. I worked seven days a week. I liked what I was doing, and I was good at it.

My career grew steadily from that point on. I moved nine times in nine years, always looking for the next hotel. The next opportunity. The next chance to do more in the industry I loved. Sometimes, I didn't even know what I was getting paid until the first check came—I just took the jobs they offered. Part of the allure was that I enjoyed working in corporate business and group hotels. The nightclubs, the four-star restaurants—those places and people who frequented them seemed to me to embody the epitome of success.

It's clear to me now: on that first incentive trip I won as a paperboy, while riding in that bumpy bus on the way to San Diego as an eleven-year-old, I tasted what it was like to win. Every year after that and even until recently, I was looking to win in the traditional sense—promotions, performance awards, advancement opportunities, and raises. My life seemed to be everything I wanted—or, at least, what I thought I wanted at the time. Ultimately, though, the traditional trappings of success would not be what made me happy.

BROADER LESSONS

Companies today want A-players, exceptionally talented and motivated people they can count on. Feeding into the narrow worldview of long ago, though, isn't the way to get the best out of people today.

Employees do their best work when they're inspired—that fact hasn't changed. *What* inspires them, though, has. In the era of Mr. Sannes's lecture, many people didn't take jobs because they wanted to contribute—they took jobs because they were *supposed* to take jobs and make money. Simple as that.

Looking back, I often ask myself *why* I moved so many times in nine short years, creating distance from my wife, leaving friends, and relocating my kids. I know it was because I was inspired. Inspired by the opportunity to be General Manager of the Year. To learn and master the industry that was fueling my ability to buy a home, have new cars, build a wine collection, and so on. I wanted to be the youngest general manager in the history of the company—and I was. Many in my generation shared this view of success. Some of us made good on our attempts to reach it, and some didn't.

The same is true of employees today: just like having a company car doesn't make you a great employee, wanting to work and travel remotely doesn't make you a great remote employee. What does? If your work inspires you, you're bound to bring more passion and dedication to your profession. The truth is that inspiration is hard to find in a cubicle. We bring forth our best selves when we are fully activated as human beings, not just as workers. In these moments, all your diverse energies and abilities are recognized and summoned. When you're fully activated, and that activation is countered in part with opportunities you're given to do work—which, in most cases, is a necessity of life—you're infinitely more balanced. More at peace. More engaged. Better.

If you're reading this book, and you think you already sufficiently inspire and encourage your employees by incentivizing them with perks like extra vacation days or casual Fridays, think again. Ask yourself: What is your number one challenge when it comes to personnel? Finding and retaining top talent is always in the top three responses. If you answered similarly, it's clear that how you're attracting and motivating your team isn't working—and I relate.

After I left the hotel industry and started my own digital marketing agency, I sought out the brightest, youngest talent. I looked at their level of experience and at how loyal I thought they'd be. If they had six jobs in one year, I moved them to the "no" pile, believing that moving from one job to another was a sign of failure, instability, or an attempt to hide flaws. Only now do I realize how wrong I was. All those opportunities and different experiences are points of pride—a deliberate tactic for the super talented and a nod to their vision, understanding, clarity, and agility. VUCA Prime provides a telling glimpse into the whole person (not just the highlight reel).

Once, I interviewed a woman for a position that involved writing, designing, and developing websites. She came to me as a stacked player—that is, one person with the capabilities of many. She had gone to school and completed personal training to achieve her stacked player status. The interview was excellent until I asked her what was then one of my favorite interview questions.

"Where do you see yourself in five years?" I asked.

I wanted her to say she wanted my job. That she wanted to be CEO. That she was in it for the long haul.

She didn't.

"I want to be a chiropractor," she said.

Silence. In retrospect, I was giving her the Mr. Sannes silent treatment.

I didn't hire the woman, and now, I recognize it was a huge mistake. She would have been a terrific addition to my team, even for the short term. Here's what I ignored: the average length of time an individual stays at a job right now is four and a half years, and that's on the high side. Those in charge of hiring today—just as I was doing a few short years ago—are often sitting in offices adorned with certificates for longevity of service. They've given up holidays, missed major family events, and skipped taking a vacation because projects came up—all sacrifices for the sake of companies (or was it?). They want people just like them, but then they also state their biggest problem is a shortage of engaged, inspired talent. It doesn't equate.

When it comes to navigating the talent wars, the old way of doing things doesn't work for the new generation. Today, employers who fail to embrace a new outlook on location independence are missing their chances to be early adopters of the Remote Revolution.

THE REMOTE REVOLUTION IN ACTION UP CLOSE

I had been in Córdoba, Argentina, for four days when I saw a message from another remote—an entrepreneur—who happened to be working from a location I'd just been to and truly loved: Medellín, Colombia. The two-sentence Slack post popped up into the right-hand corner of my laptop screen, reading, "Looking for two talented individuals with a history in start-ups and marketing. Let me know if you know anyone." That message was from an über talented remote named Mike. I responded immediately.

"Mike, you're in one of my favorite countries. I'm the remote you need. You don't have to look any further. I'd love to work with you." The tables had turned. Actually, I had turned them on myself. I was applying for a remote opportunity rather than talking to applicants.

Mike and I talked for about fifteen minutes, and I came to learn his partner was based in an agency in the UK. Within thirteen hours from the initial post, I was on a conference call with Mike's partner—the founder of an accelerated innovation start-up—talking about inspirations, life goals, our personal missions, and how he wanted to affect positive change and influence the lives of one billion people in the next twenty years. He had my undivided attention. Later, we discussed the parameters of the project, and he offered me a "talent agreement"—their innovative, warm term for contract. I was excited by the idea of helping turn an idea on a napkin into a company, working on a customer relationship management (CRM), an automation platform, a website, and a marketing plan—all with three and a half weeks to launch day. Exhilarated, I signed. It was a win-win. As part of a network gig team, Mike's company was hiring me for about one-fourth of my going US rate, because I would be living and working in Medellín, Colombia. Plus, I was a stacked player.

Next, I hopped on a flight and surrounded myself with other remotes who had been working on the project. Mike and I grinded through eighteen-hour days. It wasn't easy, but the company LEAPS™ had a very successful launch. After my three-week talent engagement ended, I reflected on the sacrifices and successes I had experienced on that project and the myriad before it. Most importantly, I reflected on whom I'd met along the way and how I was living the ideal remote life.

The first eleven months of my remote year, I was the one looking to pull talented individuals into *my* projects. It was a successful plan, as one of the key elements of the culture-driven tribe and family of remotes and location-independent talent is community. My last month, ironically, I had a new opportunity—to be called *into* a project by someone I didn't know, and that someone was in another country. My experience of working with Mike and his company solidified just how far I'd come. I was personally living in the Future of Work.

WE'RE ALL IN THE PEOPLE BUSINESS

There is an entire generation that will not (and does not) look forward to having their own desks in their own offices with their own names emblazoned on business cards and wall plaques. They have a new set of motivations, ones attributed to what they deem as truly important in their lives.

My many years in the hospitality industry taught me not only about business but also about the psychology of human behavior. There, I learned that no matter what industry you hail from, we're all in the people business. Ironically, the insights I took from my corporate career primed me for what was to come, making me more receptive to the concepts behind the remote movement—namely, that your employees are your guests, too. The number one rule of the hotel business? You always take care of your guests.

CHAPTER 2

BEHIND THE SCENES, BEYOND THE BOARDROOM

Earlier in this book, I mentioned that Tyler and I were on a quest to see the amazing griffon vulture while living in Serbia.

Tyler, thirty-one years old, was born in Missouri and spent the first few years in a small town of Bolivar, population a click over ten thousand. I can say unequivocally the chances of Tyler and I ever meeting, much less becoming roommates and very good friends were worse odds than he and I getting struck by lightning at the same time in different parts of the world. But guess what? Lightning did strike Tyler and me, but that lightning's name is Jenna Winn.

Jenna's official title is program leader. Her title couldn't come close to matching her role with Remote Year. Jenna was expected to be omnipresent the entire year for all seventy-two of us. Her smile and attitude became the heart and soul of our entire group. This is no ordinary smile either. It was ear-to-ear every day on the twenty-eight-year-old from Mattapoisett, Massachusetts. If you question *my* enthusiasm for Jenna's felicitous style, it is well documented in Pharrell Williams's twenty-four-hour video *Happy*. Jenna is the star of the minute from 4:52 p.m. to 4:53 p.m.

Why is this important to note in a book about the Remote Revolution? Because Jenna far exceeded the expectations of seventy-two very strong type A personality location-independent professionals *for a year*. Her counterpart, Aline from the Netherlands, was equally talented and brought focus and creativity to the team. This woman executed on every detail with precision and confidence. She was not afraid to play the role adviser/decision maker when issues came up involving conflict. I loved her ability to be direct and candid. Together, another great example of Team Genius.

Why take your time to explain the behind-the-scenes

support for remotes? Because it proves that a very small, talented team like Aline and Jenna can provide the support and programming for *more than seventy professionals*. Think about it. Does your office run with only two people who understand logistics that include all travel, housing, and office requirements, attitudes, complaints, global safety issues, airline strikes, and any of a thousand other things that can and will arise while taking care of seventy-two people living and working around the world, and *then* offer 24-7 support? Of course it doesn't. But if you have seventy-two inspired, talented individuals, you can assign a much smaller, equally talented team to keep them focused and productive, especially if they are the caliber of Aline and Jenna.

One of Jenna's primary responsibilities was to pair remotes with other remotes as roommates. Try to imagine putting together people you barely knew yourself—co-eds from all over the world with different skills and expectations. Roughly every thirty days for a year, Jenna would put the roommate assignments together like a jigsaw puzzle. As remotes within the program, we had a lot of autonomy. We worked when we wanted, we slept when we wanted, and came and went however we wanted. But whom we lived with? That assignment was in the hands of Jenna. Masterfully, month after month, country after country, I saw her make amazing choices—choices that sometimes seemed unusual at first. Like a lightning strike, Tyler and I found ourselves as roommates our very first month.

NEW AGE ODD COUPLE

Neil Simon, American playwright, screenwriter, and author, wrote the original Broadway play titled *The Odd Couple* more than fifty years ago. The iconic lead characters have become legions of American pop culture. The plot concerns two mismatched roommates: the uptight Felix Ungar and the easygoing Oscar Madison.

Fast-forward to May 28, 2016. I stood at the bar in the Delta Sky Lounge at the JFK airport in New York. I had about an hour and a half before my plane to Prague was scheduled to depart. A month or so before, Remote Year published tabs and tabs of valuable information pertaining to our yearlong adventure, and the private portal was available online and only accessible to the Remote Year staff and those who had been selected to live and work around the world together. The portal included advance briefs on the upcoming cities we would be living in, details on our workspaces, transportation instructions, and the all-important accommodations list. This list was treated like the honor roll list your principal would put up in school or the "who made the team" roster posted by coaches before the season started. Each month, there was great anticipation that mounted before the list was published on our portal. We never knew who our roommate or roommates were going to be until a week before travel day.

I introduced myself to Tyler via Facebook Messenger four days before we were scheduled to depart for Prague. It went like this:

Facebook Messenger 5/22/2016 8:15 p.m.

Me: Hey, Tyler, it's John Elston. Looks like we are roommates in Prague...looking forward to meeting you. I have NOT packed yet!!! :(

Tyler: Looking forward to meeting you as well. My kettle unfortunately isn't going to make it with me, but if I can find one to buy locally we should have a nice setup for making coffee and tea I'm bringing along. :)

Tyler: I have been packed for a week. Anything I can do to help you figure out what to pack?

Me: Thanks, but I have no idea. I might take you up on that in the next forty-eight hours.

Me: Are you flying out of JFK on Saturday?

Tyler: Yeah. I fly from San Antonio to JFK in the morning and then I hang around JFK for seven hours until my flight DL0411 from JFK to Prague at 8:00 p.m. Eastern.

Me: Nice! Checking my flt now. I am on the same flt. Let's meet in the Delta Club Lounge.

Tyler: Absolutely. I'm sure we'll discover a lot of new things together. :)

That is how this Odd Couple relationship started—and that's how it has continued for the last year and a half. He packs a week in advance, and I pack the night before. He knows the airline, flight number, time of departure, and probably the make and model of the plane we will be flying on, and I am not sure if I have booked my flight and so on and so forth.

I point out these differences because I want to share that successful location-independent professions come in all shapes and sizes. We all have quirks and shortcomings, but we also have our individual strengths. When lightning strikes, capture it, embrace it, and turn it into positive energy. Even though Tyler and I are such different people, we share successful remote qualities: our work always comes first, we have high capacities for work, and we have extremely high work ethics.

If you only hire location-independent professionals with these three qualities, you will be way ahead of the game and your competitors.

EXPERIENCE FIRST

The *experience-first* mindset on business and living I've cultivated as an embedded remote—that is, a permanently location-independent professional working for one company—might seem like a far cry from my old, traditional business mindset. I used to be solely focused on the next step; now, I'm focused on how work is a meaningful part of a whole person, not just a vehicle to reach the next rung on the corporate ladder.

The kicker? It turns out, those two mindsets aren't as different as they seem.

The hospitality industry is about making customers feel at home. I was required to focus on the little things. Does the guest want the newspaper at their front door? Do they like rooms close to the elevator, or a particular item for breakfast? It's all about making customers feel cared for. It's about making them feel at home, even though they're away from home.

Sometimes, the customer would choose to spend their

disposable income on an *experience*—travel and the hotel stay. Other times, though, the customer *had* to travel. There's a difference. The latter—the majority, I would argue—would rather be home, and they dislike the fact they're away. Great hospitality is about filling those gaps as well as possible. The common denominator? Experience makes or breaks it all—proof of my greater theory on the Future of Work.

Like much of life, hiring remote talent parallels a deposit-and-withdrawal system. By making deposits—in the way of great experiences—companies can make up for the inevitable withdrawals like reductions in primary benefit packages. And if they've made enough deposits and the remote has opportunity for experiences outside of their job description, the withdrawals are easier to stomach. Remotes' experience is about balancing the relationship budget. If you approach recruiting with a remote-focus and experience-first mindset, you're not providing just another perk—you're changing the game.

I received an interesting question following a talk I gave to dozens of top, cultured HR policy makers and leaders.

"John, how do we get our hiring mangers behind this revolution of remote professionals?" the audience member asked.

My answer?

"Don't let them get behind it!"

The crowd stared back at me with wide eyes. I felt like my response sucked the air out of the room.

I quickly shouted again, with all the passion I've been known to exude when speaking on this topic.

"Don't let them get behind it! Put them in front of it!"

Think about it. Within your organization, there are already trusted, loyal, driven employees who would love to be the next Jenna or Aline. These are current players already on your team who understand your culture. They have worked hard to prove to you and others that they can be trusted. There is a great chance that in-house superstars want to work remotely and maybe even take responsibility for providing the necessary support to manage an entire remote team.

A WIN-WIN

Leading with a remote experience plan is not the norm for many businesses today. To recruit and retain top talent, instead, many companies offer big, bursting benefit packages. The only problem is that those aren't the benefits employees—especially young, hungry, high-performing employees—truly want.

A typical benefit package often looks like this: one-week paid vacation per year plus sick days, dollar-for-dollar match for 401(k), and the choice between a partially compensated PPO or HMO health insurance plan. Oh, and maybe—just maybe—a company meal or cup of coffee here or there.

Many HR and business leaders take the position that these policies are non-negotiable. They're simply how the company operates—take it or leave it. These so-called "desirable" prerequisites, though, don't interest talented location-independent employees.

Companies need to adapt. Here are some ideas companies can use to gain an advantage when recruiting top remotes. What they'll get in return is commitment, stellar work delivered on time, accountability, transparency, and pictures—lots of pictures.

- *Pay 100 percent of passport fees and provide complete internal documentation for all visa requests.*
- *Provide an allowance for travel gear and a backpack complete with all the essentials your employees will need to be effective and productive.*

- *Offer a deferred start, such that your employee begins the first of the month, but they don't have to report to work. Instead, you pay them for the first month before they work a day. Why? Remote workers need time to get acquainted with their surroundings before you can expect them to perform. Plus, you'll have problems paying them to see sunrises and sunsets, because you'll know you've hired the right employee who will work hard and get the job done.*
- *Replace time cards and business cards with an Uber card and a WeWork membership card.*

Companies should consider two independently designed benefit packages: one tailored for the remote worker and one for those working in a traditional office landscape, offering varying degrees of the above benefits. To further expand on the importance of vetting remote employees, I recommend employers also develop requirements for remotes applying for such sought-after opportunities. Eventually, hiring location-independent employees will become more challenging for hiring managers. As the Remote Revolution continues to gain popularity, less talented applicants will attempt to gain the status as a qualified remote worker. Diligence on behalf of the employer will be the key to keeping this elite status of *genuinely* qualified remotes at the top of the talent pool. The following are measurable achievements and requirements that could be included in the qualification process.

- An experienced traveler with a specific number of days living and working abroad within the last six months.
- A tally of days the remote has checked into a communal workspace like WeWork. WeWork requires sign-in protocols that record members as they come and go from their spaces.
- An adherence to weekend relocations, as remotes should understand that one of the expectations is if they decide to move to another location, the move must be completed on a weekend to avoid any interference with company workflow or deadlines.
- A track record of selecting a safe location is a top priority, as is selecting a location with reliable Wi-Fi.

This list of remote requirements will naturally expand as the number of companies leading the Remote Revolution starts to develop their best practices.

The bottom line? The world's best talent would start to not only line up to work for a company with policies like the one outlined above; they'd also tell all their colleagues and friends about the opportunity, likely sharing it to social sites like LinkedIn, Twitter, Facebook, and Instagram. In short, the talent floodgates would begin to open.

Why? When employers embrace a remote experience-driven employee approach, it brings out the best in their team. It's common sense that the more energetic and engaged an employee is, the better he or she will perform. Overall, remote workers are grateful for the opportunity to live where they please, work while feeling personally fulfilled, and they'll perform continually so as to not squander that chance. They understand what it's like to be fully activated both personally and professionally. They're not the only one who benefits—their company, too, gets perks in return, like higher productivity, higher energy, and stronger performance.

FROM THERE TO HERE

My current vantage point on the power of leveraging location-independent professionals to win the talent war hasn't always been something I understood or supported. I *have*, however, always focused on providing a positive experience for the teams I've built. I've had my eyes on one key prize: get employee experience right. What does it mean to get it right? I am the first to admit that my natural leadership style is to sell, build consensus, and gain ownership from those involved in the decisions that affect the team's daily experiences. But for some reason, again, I will admit that for years with my own agency, some topics weren't up for discussion or vote with my teams. One of those was from where they could physically perform their work.

CHAPTER 3

A RUDE AWAKENING

In 2010, my employment agreement with Sunstone/Interstate Hotels & Resorts was ending, and we were in the middle of a deep recession—arguably the worst business economy in the history of the United States. Unemployment was very high.

The parent company, IHR, was forcing a consolidation of my fifty-five-plus corporate employees based in Southern California. They eventually got what they wanted; we laid off more than 85 percent of my team and closed the office.

My business partner and I, plus a half-dozen other employees, were offered a chance to stay on board—but they wanted us on the East Coast. He and I decided to walk away. He stayed in the hotel business, joining another hospitality company. As for me? My son was still in high school, and I didn't want to move my family from Southern California. There was another reason, too. Always opportunistic, I saw a business opportunity in a segment I'd been honing throughout my career—digital marketing. So, in the world's worst economy, I walked away from a very high six-figure income to start my own agency.

Why digital marketing? In my twenty-eight years working in the hospitality industry, I built an operations background that paired nicely with my intuitive ability to sell. As my career progressed, so did the digital world around me. For example, in 2000, I started my tenure at Sunstone as the vice-president of sales and quickly moved up the ranks to run the sales and marketing for the entire company. During that time, we had a traditional sales operation with national and regional sales teams—in short, it was a "boots on the ground, knock on the door, make the cold call" strategy.

At the same time, it was evident social media was starting to become a necessity for businesses—as were interactive website experiences and online booking. I saw that we needed to break into that space. Digital wasn't new to most of the world, but it was new to the antiquated hotel business—a fact I realized during my tenure at Sunstone/ IHR.

While there, we started focusing on building websites, mapping social media strategies, and improving our online booking system so we could move share from our competitors. Major brands were sticking with their traditional sales strategies and tactics. My official job description was standard: grow market share and increase revenue. My mantra? Heads in beds, serve hot food hot and cold food cold, and fill up every room possible. It was simple—except that it wasn't. My real value to the company was ideally to optimize the company for the digital evolution.

Although I was jumping into the digital space with both feet, I didn't have the team or the capacity in-house to complete tasks like optimizing websites, building social media campaigns, and revamping web presence. So I outsourced the work to various agencies. "Stacked agencies"—ones that perform *everything* digital—didn't exist yet, and it was frustrating and inefficient managing multiple agencies at once. I knew there had to be a better way, so I made one. Focusing on training instead of outsourcing, my team learned how to design, develop, and optimize websites, write content, and eventually lead hotels into the world of responsive websites and aggregating social media.

I started firing the agencies one at a time. The goal was to be independent of outside agencies for key deliverables.

Over those five years, I was building and creating my future digital agency without even knowing it. By the time I left the hospitality industry and launched Yo!Dog Marketing, I knew I had a strong business plan that would allow me to provide that service to other companies.

Business during those early months at Yo!Dog was slow. At first, that was partially by design. My plan was to launch and make the agency successful without picking the low hanging fruit and calling on the contacts and prior business partners I had worked with in the past. It was part of the *scale* plan. Instead, I wanted to take more of an uphill approach and solicit new clients who may have known of the hotels I ran in the past and maybe they even competed against me. The goal? To make them fans and new clients.

It worked. Slowly, I built the confidence of first-time clients and, quite honestly, my own confidence in the process. I found the sweet spot, identifying which sized clients fit best in my model. I learned the hard way. I spent just as much time and energy on a client with one hotel as I did on a client with seven hotels. I learned that clients with more than thirty-five hotels would listen and agree with me that they needed my services, but they almost always decided to build out their own platforms or extend their existing systems. Once I figured out my value in the eyes of the client, I targeted clients with seven to thirty-five assets.

Still, we experienced many pain points in the first year after our launch. Looking back, though, what I got in return for starting a business in the middle of a recession was human capital. I hired phenomenal talent. It was 2010—a tough time to be a college graduate, but a good time to hire them. Why? It had always been common-place for midlevel graduates—the top 25 to 40 percent or so of major schools—to stretch out their educations, moving to MBA programs or even just living at home and slowly looking for work. In that awful economy, however, a large portion of the elite students—the top 1 to 5 percent—were leaving school without job offers. My digital agency model depended on high-performing, young graduates. Fortunately for me, the poor economic climate gave my brand-new agency the rare opportunity to hire the best and brightest. And I did.

In fact, having the opportunity to hire elite graduates and bring a couple superstars with me from my Southern California team was a large part of my decision to walk away from big money in the hospitality industry to enter the unknown—an unknown, by the way, where I'd be the last one paid. I knew non-remuneration to myself could last a couple of years with a start-up. I knew I was going to burn through my savings, bootstrapping this agency, and risking all my hard-earned money from the last twenty-eight years. I also knew I was making the right choice, and having such an unprecedented access to human capital was the final piece I needed to convince myself to start Yo!Dog Marketing. We're still going strong seven years later, but that doesn't mean it was always easy.

Finding and recruiting top talent in 2010 was simple. Retaining them? That's another story.

TALENT TROUBLE

I was fortunate to hire all these top college graduates and experienced professionals, but I didn't realize retaining them would be such a struggle. At first, they didn't mind driving to my sleepy, funky beach town of less than sixty-four thousand people in San Clemente, California. My talented team came from Boston University, UCLA, the University of Texas, the University of Utah, and the like. They didn't mind commuting into the agency office. They just wanted the work. They *needed* the work.

During the next two to three years, though, everything changed.

I chose San Clemente as the home base for Yo!Dog selfishly. I wanted to be close to home, and the property value was solid. I tried to build a Facebook-esque experience for my employees to compensate for the out-of-the-way location. At the time, we had nine employees, a 5,500-square-foot space, a bistro, a couch room, a studio, and a gym. Oh, and a Nerf gun armory. Everyone loved it—or at least I thought they did. Truthfully, I had no idea what my employees wanted deep down. I just figured if Facebook was doing it, I should be doing it.

We soon grew to twenty employees, but then things weren't like I envisioned they'd be. Several A-players left the agency, putting pressure on the existing A-team. The average age of my team members was around twenty-six years old. San Clemente is nice, but my team was driving to LA every weekend to go to clubs and nice restaurants. They wanted entertainment, concerts, dating, and options. They needed more than my small city could offer, and guess what? They started getting job offers from larger cities like San Diego, Los Angeles, and San Francisco.

One day, the director of the social media division came to my office—an A-player and someone I truly relied on in the agency.

"Boss," she said, "I love working here. I enjoy my role and I'm learning a lot."

I could feel the dreaded "but" coming, and it did.

"BUT I need more of a life. I spend so much time coming and going to and from the office. On the weekends, I drive to LA to see friends."

I kept my mouth closed despite my propensity to interrupt her. Still, though, not blurting out what I wanted to say didn't keep my racing mind from thinking it.

What could be better than this? I wondered. I didn't understand. I had gone to great lengths to foster and build an agency and a space that felt good to step into. But I failed to see my business through the eyes of the real people—the people who were taking care of our clients. The people who were creating our next deliverables. The people who made us who we were as an agency. It wasn't just the twenty-four-year-old stars; my inner circle was feeling it too, including my talented vice-president overseeing product development, my confidant/business manager, our senior developer, and even my own daughter. It was staring me in the face every day. They had priorities and needs that I didn't acknowledge.

From my corner high-tech office, I focused on my superstar performer who was, I could tell, about to pose a question.

"What do you think about me moving to Los Angeles and working from home in LA?"

I didn't even have to think about it. My response came rapid-fire, almost automatic.

"Absolutely not," I said. "We are building a culture. We are a team. Our clients expect us to be here when they need us."

Looking back, I ask myself, *What was I thinking?* Even writing it makes me sick to my stomach. But that's what happened. Then three days later, she gave me her resignation. She said she was tired of not having balance in her life, tired of sitting in traffic en route to LA every weekend and feeling exhausted every Monday morning. She was talented, and she loved both her work and the agency. Still, she didn't want to live to work, but to *work to live*. Experiences. Adventures. A new city with lots of options.

I balked. I couldn't lose an A-player! So I did what I thought would fix the situation: I offered her more money—even some profit sharing and equity. Always polite and respectful, she said she would think about it and let me know. I confided in our business manager and told her about the offer I had made, and she looked me in the eyes.

"She won't take that," my business manager said.

"Oh, of course she will!" I replied.

However, my business manager was spot-on, as always. My superstar gave me ample notice the next day and took a job at an agency in LA.

I didn't learn my lesson when I lost her, but it slowly began to sink in as more of my best employees followed suit. There was a pattern—people would be happy at first, then get tired after about eighteen months. Everyone wanted to live in cities that offered what was important to them. They wanted to live in neighborhoods where they could afford a place with a backyard for their kids to play or have enough money left after paying their bills so they could take weekend trips. My employees *wanted* to work, but long commutes to offices weren't where they wanted to spend their time.

Believe it or not, these weren't just millennials I am writing about. They weren't employees who felt entitled. They were parents. They were young. They were talented. And I lost many of them, including my senior developer who moved to Florida for family and medical reasons. At the time, she had been with me almost three years and was solely a developer; she rarely needed to interact with clients or people at the office. Still, when she asked if she could work remotely, I shook my head and said, "No."

"We're building an agency, and this is how we work," I told her. "You can't work from Florida; we're going to have to replace you." It hurt, but it's what I believed at the time.

After I lost three or four of my best people to competitors in gateway cities or other moves, my eyes started to open, not all the way, though—at least not enough to change my policies. Then, I stopped getting A-level talent between 2013 and 2015. It seemed as if all applicants had similar questions: Do you allow people to work from home? Do you allow people to take off every Friday? Can we share workloads and cover each other?

Although my stance on remote work had softened, it was still there. I said, "No, absolutely not." I wouldn't budge. It was hard to teach an old dog at Yo!Dog new tricks.

THE FINAL BLOW: LET'S DECENTRALIZE

Finally, I looked through our customers' eyes and realized that because my ability to retain our talented team had slipped, so had Yo!Dog's performance. We weren't getting work done on time, and we had to turn down new projects. I'd always taken pride in our reference list and the fact that we'd never lost a single client, but that soon changed. We started to lose business, not because we were unresponsive or charged too much, but because our work suffered after losing team members. Losing talent had other effects, too. We wasted inordinate amounts of time hiring staff. It was becoming harder and harder to focus on growing the agency, because we were spending so much time recruiting and training new hires.

Then, the last straw happened. One of our designers, Andrew, walked into my office one morning.

"Hey, John. It's taking me forty-five minutes to an hour—one way—to drive into the office. I live in Huntington Beach," he said. "I am so much more productive when I work remotely, and it's a better use of my time."

He then went on to explain that he loved to surf, had a new girlfriend, and really wished I would consider the benefits. What I now understand after being a remote professional is his life had other priorities. Working toward the goal of becoming the creative director at the agency was taking a back seat within that balance. He also wanted the experience of getting up and surfing in the morning and being able to occasionally grab an early dinner with his girlfriend.

I sat there, listening and feeling like a beaten warrior. Finally, it was starting to sink in. What he was saying made so much sense. I rocked back and forth in my chair, silent.

Then I said, "You know what, Andrew? That's going to be OK. We're going to work out a plan for you to work a couple of days from home," I said. "Let's give it a try."

Two days later, I met with my COO and told him we needed to pivot the agency's philosophy on remote work. Although I had almost a year left on our lease, I knew the decision to decentralize the office was the right one. I wasn't completely convinced it would make the agency better, but I was willing to give it a try. I knew some of my team members had expressed interest in remote work but not all. Would some of them view the decision as a weakening of the agency? Would they question the validity of their positions? Would they be upset?

I called a meeting in the bistro for the next morning. Our bistro meetings had always been about celebration—winning a new client or award, announcing a promotion, and so forth. Expecting the same, my employees bounded in, upbeat and bustling. I, on the other hand, was nervous as I tried to prepare them for the bomb I was about to drop.

"What I have to tell you will probably disappoint most of you," I said. "But I want you to understand that it's not a reflection on you or the agency—we've never been more profitable or grown at a faster pace. Here's the deal: as of next Thursday, we're closing the office."

I went on to explain that they still had their jobs; the only difference was they could work from anywhere. For most, they would be able to work from home. I held my breath, expecting disappointment and concern. I got none of that. Seconds later, Andrew stood up and clapped.

It was a scene reminiscent of the Robert Redford movie, *Brubaker*—one clap, then one more stood up. Another. Soon, everyone was standing and clapping. They were thrilled, and I was fighting raw emotion.

"You guys heard me, right? The office is shutting down," I said. "We'll set you up with laptops and everything you need to work remotely."

From that day forward, in summer 2015, I felt a shift in momentum, productivity, attitude, and openness at Yo!Dog. The agency was five years old, but I had never seen employees so open to working hard, and even late. They were inspired.

The COO and I went into the office every day for the next six to eight months until the lease ran out. We were two people in this massive space, using remote-friendly collaboration tools like Skype, GoToMeeting, and Zoom while on conference calls with our team. Instead of clients coming to us, we'd visit them—a setup that felt more personal, anyway. It soon became evident that the decision to decentralize wasn't just a good decision—it was a *great* decision.

Soon after, our bottom line started to improve. Costs had shrunk. We were using less utilities, and fewer expense reports were turned in. Soon, we needed a developer, and our ad mentioned our most important policy—you can work from anywhere.

Suddenly, we got A-level applications again. This time, though, they were from all over the world—Chicago, Dubai, Thailand, and India, to name a few. It was like the good old days when college grads were knocking down the door but better.

When the lease ran out, I figured if you can't beat 'em, join 'em. I started working from home and planning trips to meet with my employees for one-on-one reviews and collaborations. The rest is history. Today, my senior web developer lives in India. My reputation management leader lives in Massachusetts. The president lives five hundred miles away from San Clemente. It doesn't matter where they kick ass—but they all kick ass.

I used to think inspiration meant giving my employees more money or hiring a barista to bring their craft coffee to their cubicle. Wrong! I now know inspiration is allowing them to work from anywhere, at any time.

After decentralization, the next step was sending people abroad. Then, *I* went abroad. This was the Future of Work, and I wanted to be at the forefront. That brings me to where I am today.

If Andrew hadn't woken me up, we would have kept losing our A-players. Our customers would have suffered. My margins would have shrunk as I would have paid higher prices for lower quality work. Bottom line? The decision to decentralize and encourage remote work saved my business.

THE CALL

Today, we live in what I call the "insta" world. On Instagram and other social media platforms, everything happens *now*—and that's not necessarily a bad thing. Instead, it means you can learn, discover, create, share, and connect from anywhere. Want to become a sommelier? Take a quick class online to learn how to pair wine with food. You can learn how to do anything—make beer, write a book, become a photographer, volunteer. These are the kinds of experiences people want in their lives these days, and it makes them light up inside.

Don't get me wrong—"insta" doesn't mean easy. Remotes do understand they will need to work for a living. They live in a different world, though, and they're good at multitasking and accomplishing things quickly with technology. The up-and-coming talent doesn't want to wait twenty years for a promotion because they know they don't have to. Today, young people care less about traditional wealth accumulation and ladder climbing. Instead, they want a visceral life experience.

I've seen the shift for myself. As I've traveled the world, I've watched my peers get involved locally. It's in their genes. They want to learn, grow, and give back wherever they are. Companies spend tons of money fostering similar "inspiring" experiences for team members, but location-independent employees often seek them out on their own.

As of this writing, eighteen of my former traveling cohorts are spending six days this month building a house with three local people in Lima, Peru. They are moving independently throughout the world, helping others, giving back, and making a difference.

The Remote Revolution allows employees to choose both their best life experience and their best work experience, not one or the other. It's a game changer.

I put on the silver Anchor bracelet the day before I left on my journey around the world. It symbolized a new season of my life. I felt eager and alive. I was laden with hope, excitement, imaginings, and aspirations. Side by side with the peaceful reminder of where I came from, the latitude and longitude bracelet (a gift from my mom) was stamped with the coordinates of my hometown.

The iconic poem "Advice from a Tree" by Ilan Shamir was abbreviated and hand-drawn by my cousin's wife, Nikki, and given to me as a traveling mantra. It lived on four continents, in eight countries, and in twelve cities.

Will the real Tyler Taboada please stand up? As a remote you learn never to say goodbye to your friends when they leave. You just say, "See you soon!" One Tyler could never be enough, so we all donned our T. T. masks at his surprise going away party in Bogotá, Colombia. Tyler was promoted to the Europe and Africa Experience Director with RY.

Aline Yntema and Jenna Winn, in London, respond to seeing a photo in the viewfinder of another remote's camera.

I took this photo on one of my many morning walks in Prague, Czech Republic. Known as the "Dancing House," it is set on a property of great historical significance. Its site was the location of a house destroyed by the US bombing of Prague in 1945. The architect's original idea was of a building consisting of two parts, static and dynamic ("yin and yang"), which were to symbolize the transition of Czechoslovakia from a communist regime to a parliamentary democracy.

As important as community is to location-independent professionals, I often choose to explore alone on my free weekends. While living in Lima, Peru I couldn't resist the planes, trains, and buses it took to get me to the Inca Trail and then Machu Picchu.

Work for reward: Jake and I choose to laugh instead of cry in the backseat as Danny catapults us off of a massive dune in the Sahara Desert.

Boys to men: Jake, Brian, and Chase celebrate their climb to the top of a dune, deep in the Sahara Desert. Sand boarding was an unexpected treat our first night in the desert.

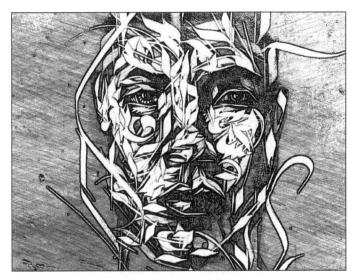

It did not take long to figure out that Valencia, Spain, is home to some
of the best street art in the world (see more at johnelston.com).

Chase and Stu cool off in the Draa River in Zagora, North Africa.

Tyler Duzan outside the Ledena Cave in the Uvac Canyon, Serbia

Madhatters Lish and Ee Yeen commandeer traditional
London lids on a weekend walking tour.

Dhivya and I shared as much Shisha as we did all night work-a-thons. She was one of the hardest-working remotes.

Liesbeth and Stephan introduced me to the festival scene in Northamptonshire, UK. The three of us performed as invited artists with the Natural Born Storytellers.

One of the hottest talents I worked with was Eddie Contento.
He was twenty-three years old when we met.

CHAPTER 4

THE AHA MOMENT

The light went on. It hit me like a ton of bricks. It was my aha moment. Any number of metaphors would have fit the moment when my friend Sean said the words, "Remote Year." The first time I heard those two words put together was in January 2016. I was sitting in a rooftop bar in Laguna Beach having some drinks with the twins, Ashley and Amy, and Ashley's husband, Sean. We had become friends over the years after working together. I don't get to hang out with them often enough, but when I do, we always seem to start kicking around my crazy ideas or discussing what I'm creating or considering. Sean is a smart guy who holds down a corporate marketing job for the country's largest family-run fitness company, but his capacity for work is larger. Outside his full-time gig, he always has his hands in several things, whether he studies the algorithms on Instagram to grow his audience for his e-book on how to become a social influencer, producing content for their successful hiking blog, or talking through his early adopter idea on how to build a philanthropic platform where investors can assign their investment dividends to philanthropic groups of their choice. On top of these types of ideas, Sean is always in training for the next half marathon, triathlon, or mud run.

I am always ten to fifteen minutes late whenever I meet Sean. What Sean and the girls *don't* know is I'm always late to meet them because I'm in the parking lot stretching and getting loosened up for the confabulation session that is about to proceed. When we get together, Sean is either pummeling me with performance questions or specific interview-style questions like, "Describe the best meal you've eaten this month," or "Tell me the exact moment you decided to sell your car and why." Tonight, as the girls sipped their sauvignon blancs, Sean stared at me over the top of his craft beer.

"So what are you going to do next in your life?" he asked.

I'm not kidding—when I first met him, I thought he was messing with me when he would start conversations with questions like that. But he wasn't. I swear he sits around and premeditates these questions to get even with me for showing up ten to fifteen minutes late when we get together.

"Funny you should ask," I said. "I'm closing a deal with one of the world's best car manufacturers to drive and live around the country." I went on to explain that I had pitched an idea that would allow me to go where I wanted to go, work where I wanted to work, and live where I wanted to live—whenever I wanted. I was going to take my dog, Kevin, and curate content along the away that could be used by the car manufacturer to promote their world-class Sprinter, a fully outfitted small home office on wheels. I called it a land jet so I could pre-frame whomever I was telling about the idea and leave them with a visual about what the vehicle looked like without having to explain lengthy details. The plan was to live anywhere in the country and run my agency from wherever it motivated me.

Sean interrupted and said, "I have a friend I went to school with at Brown. She is doing something similar, but she's doing it all over the world." I am not generally the person sitting around the table being told to think bigger. But, in essence, that's what Sean was saying. Why limit myself to the United States?

"It's a yearlong program, and she's three months into her journey. Her name is Jessie." He then gave me Jessie's Facebook handle and told me to look her up. "I think the name of the start-up is Remote Year," he said.

THE MAIN EVENT: REMOTE YEAR

I cut the night short to go home and do research on the Remote Year opportunity. (Learn more about Remote Year at www.johnelston.com.) When I pulled up the website, I read:

> *Our team makes remote work simple, so that you can focus on your business.*

I devoured every page on the site. After quickly learning Remote Year was closing in on their next trip's deadline, I filled out the application and submitted it that night. I then began socially stalking the leadership team of Remote Year. One by one, I pulled up their LinkedIn profiles. I then sent personalized emails crafted with one short paragraph to each of them making sure there was at least one full sentence about something personal and relative to *their* moment. For example, I discovered Trish Kennelly, vice-president of experience, was a Clemson Tiger alumna (noted on her LinkedIn page). On her Remote Year profile page on the site, there was a picture of Trish doing the splits with a caption that read, "I have been known to drop the splits wherever I am in the world."

Below is the exact email I sent Trish on January 11, 2016, at 11:10 p.m. after having drinks with Sean. Earlier that night the Clemson Tigers lost the biggest game in college football to the Alabama Tide. The score was forty to forty-five.

To: Trish Kennelly, VP of Experience, Remote Year

1/11/2016 John Elston sent the following message at 11:10 p.m.

Subject: Are You Kidding Me? So Damn Close

Trish—Sorry about the game! I was cheering for the Tigers all the way! I am a serial entrepreneur. After dedicating my professional career to hospitality and tourism, I founded Yo!Dog, a full-service digital marketing agency servicing hotels around the world. Six years later, I have positioned myself (still acting CEO) of Yo!Dog to run and grow my company while working remotely. I want to document my one-year adventure with Remote Year. I will vlog and post every day to show the world's entrepreneurs that, done right, they can grow and succeed. I WANT IN! If you drop splits in every city, I will do the happy baby pose each month! Please tell me how to keep this conversation moving forward. I have submitted my application and I am waiting to hear what's next! https://www.linkedin.com/in/johnelston Instagram @JOHNELSTON

John

To: Greg Caplin, Cofounder and CEO, Remote Year

1/12/2016 John Elston sent the following message at 2:03 a.m.

Subject: I Am Ready to Go

Greg, my name is John Elston. I am the founder/CEO of a full-service digital agency. I have worked for six years to prepare myself and my team to operate and run my company remotely. I LOVE what you have created. Remote Year is amazing. I want to be a part of your June 1, 2016, program! I have submitted my application and I'm waiting to hear about my next steps. Please let me know what I need to do to convince you and your team why I am a fantastic candidate. I am looking forward to keeping this conversation moving forward.

John Elston

To: Sam Pessin, Cofounder and COO, Remote Year

1/12/2016 John Elston sent the following message at 12:11 a.m.

Subject: LET ME IN

Sam—Congratulations to you and Greg on the success of Remote Year. I will be quick and to the point: I WANT IN. I dedicated twenty-eight years of my professional life to hospitality/leisure/tourism. Six years ago, I founded and remain today the CEO of Yo!Dog Marketing. I recently decentralized my full-service digital agency to prove that working remotely could be done in the agency environment. Sam, it's working, and now I want to take my new life on the road. I plan on leaving my agency intact and slow traveling the world. I *want* to do this with Remote Year. I *know* I will be a great ambassador for Remote Year. While running my company from your twelve amazing cities, I plan on vlogging every day and convincing the world that life is too short. PLEASE consider allowing me to join the ride in June 2016. https://www.linkedin.com/in/johnelston Instagram @JohnElston @Dog_Named_Kevin

John

As you can see, I was possessed for the first thirty-five hours after I submitted my application. I needed a way to stand out among sixty-eight thousand applicants, and I was determined to be one of the seventy-two chosen.

Fast-forward two months later. After several exchanges, interviews, and video calls, I got the email with the following words in the subject line: *Congratulations! You have been selected to live and work around the world!*

I generally follow my intuition, but I also believe in building consensus on big decisions. Not only did I not build consensus, but I had not told *one person* in my life that I was applying to get in. I was nervous; my kids were in their twenties and living their own lives, but I still wondered if they might think I was checking out for a year. Or that I was crazy. Hell, maybe I *was* crazy. But I believed in something, just like I believed my lunch box was a briefcase when I was six years old. Now I believed the Future of Work is now. I was creating my reality.

I was leaving for *a year* with little—OK, no—notice. To break the news, I took my son, daughter, and son-in-law to our favorite sushi place. I was anxious and nervous to reveal the decision I had made.

I tend to oversell things. My natural trait is to sell and promote. When I believe in something, I am enthusiastic, and my passion can be dizzying to others. I kept this in mind because my kids' buy-in was important to me, and I did not want to be selling them. I brought my Remote Year application, my interview responses, and the itinerary for the four continents, eight countries, and twelve cities. I came prepared with anything and everything that provided information about the program.

It turns out I didn't need any of that. Just like the conversation in the Yo!Dog bistro when I broke the news I was decentralizing the office, my children weren't upset or frustrated—they were excited. Supportive. Immediately, my son, a young man of few words, and my strong, not-afraid-to-speak-her-mind daughter were genuinely excited and asking questions.

In the beginning, I thought my kids were going to be upset. Instead, we had our most engaged and positive conversation in a long time.

CREATE YOUR OWN REALITY

Lish, Dhivya, and a nervous man walk into a tattoo studio in Bogotá, Colombia. (I was that nervous man.)

Lish: Hola, señor, ¿usted es el Doctor Calavera?

Dr. Calavera: Sí, ¿cómo puedo ayudarlo?

Lish: Los tres de nosotros queremos obtener el símbolo vikingo noruego para crear nuestra propia realidad.

Dr. Calavera: Pues usted ha venido al lugar correcto.

Lish: (in perfect Spanish) Hello, are you, Dr. Calavera?

Dr. Calavera: (in perfect Spanish says) Yes, I am. How can I help you?

Lish: All three of us want to get tattoos of the Norwegian Viking symbol for creating our own reality.

Dr. Calavera: Well, you have come to the right place.

My lips were perched to one side as I tried to be discreet, whispering to Dhivya, "What is she saying?" Dhivya, with her eyes as wide as saucers, looked at me anxiously and shrugged. She didn't say a word.

Dr. Calavera was the founder and artist at Dr. Calavera Tattoo Studio on Primer piso in Bogotá. Founded in 2006, the studio's logo was a mustard-colored skull and crossbones. Walking in the doors, I was convinced the Colombian man in his fifties sporting a backward ball cap, black leather vest over his bare chest, and a colorful, talon-bearing eagle tattoo the size of a large dinner platter was *not a doctor.*

Dhivya and Lish both got double-stacked chevron symbol tattoos on their right arms where their hands connect to their wrists, and each tattoo was about a quarter of an inch in length. They immediately looked great, even with the skin around the body art being bright pink from the needle pricks.

The idea for the double chevron tattoo came from Lish. She did the research and thought of a tattoo that represented the idea originally adopted by Norwegian Vikings—live or die. They believed they created their own reality through their actions. Long before Lish brought the tattoo idea to us, I had been a believer that I had indeed created my own reality, right down to that current moment.

As I stood on the black-and-white checkered floor tile trying to find the courage to lie on the red patent leather table where Dr. Calavera does his best work, I began to daydream. With my friends right next to me, I blocked out the sounds and activity of the room and focused on the energy of the moment.

When it was over, all three of us left on a natural high—sharing with one another that life truly is about the small things. We felt warm with the knowledge that from that point on, the three of us would be able to look at the permanent symbols on our bodies that represented the reality we continued to create moment by moment. The large double-stacked chevron will forever be on the bicep of my dominant left arm.

LIVE BETTER, BE BETTER

Many wait for retirement to travel and explore the world. These days, the opposite is possible. People—talented people—want to travel while they're young, for extended periods, and they can do it while making money—that is, no gap years here. Young or old, part of being a location-independent professional is creating your own reality. Likewise, companies should be turning to this talent base to create the reality of their business.

Halfway through my time with Remote Year, I realized I could make a difference and help entrepreneurs evolve to win the talent war. I wanted to show them how to do more with less. I wanted to inspire people who haven't been as lucky as me to embrace this opportunity. The entire experience was intensely gratifying to me, and I learned so much about the world and other cultures. I created successful solutions and outcomes for my business while forming incredible friendships and becoming part of a community. By living with a diverse group, I also improved my weaknesses. I became a better listener, more patient, and far more self-sustaining.

After returning from my year of living around the world, I spent Father's Day with my dad. He's strong—a man of few words, a trait that makes you pay extra attention when he speaks.

"I don't know what it is, but you're a better person today," he said. "Whatever you went through has changed you. I like it."

He could see it, and I could feel it. That proved to me my trip was as meaningful as I had thought.

REMOTE WORK: NOT JUST FOR DREAMERS

Remote work isn't just for my kids' generation. After my time with Remote Year, I know the lifestyle is possible for *anyone* who wants to live and work differently. Before Remote Year, though, I would have been skeptical. While I mainly worked with young individuals, I spent much of my time around forty- to sixty-year-old professionals, many of whom wanted to do the same thing. They'd work their asses off, then take a two-week vacation to Europe or someplace tropical. When they returned from their trips, they often needed a vacation from that vacation, because they were both worn out from cramming a year's worth of fun and relaxation into a few days *and* behind at work because they went on vacation.

It's also true that my friends are hardworking and, like many of us in the digital world, could never "turn off." Although they'd work a bit on vacation, they'd somehow still come back buried in more work. They plunged right back into the rat race, waiting for their next vacation again.

Millennials and Gen Zers have seen that level of stress and pressure on their parents, and they don't want it for themselves. They hated when Dad was twenty minutes late to horseback riding because he had to answer emails or leave vacation three days early for a board meeting. They don't *want* to live like that, working *to live* instead of working *for reward*.

Now, they don't have to.

Working for reward means prioritizing rewarding experiences. It's not about gathering the most toys, buying the most houses, or having the most lavish meals. It's about building memories and leveraging your network to accomplish a variety of things, from philanthropic endeavors to cross-professional collaboration. Without the location independence I was granted through my remote experience, how would I have crossed paths with, befriended, worked with, and learned so much from a traveling biologist from Amsterdam, an East Coast videographer, a social media expert from Chicago, an advanced

WordPress master from New York, a project manager and now best friend from Washington, DC, a recruiter from Minneapolis, and a Russian-born network engineer specializing in VoIP? Bottom line: those experiences led to friendships, work collaborations, and successes. Those experiences *were* the reward.

It doesn't matter what age we are; we all have an impulse within us to get out there and live. We shouldn't spend our whole lives sitting behind a desk, and employers shouldn't consider that matching 401(k) contributions are a sufficient "reward" for time served. It *is* a reward, just the wrong kind, and employers would be wise to stop fighting the tide and embrace it.

EXPERIENCES: BETTER WHEN SHARED

One of the most powerful and rewarding aspects of being a remote is having visitors at some point join you in the experience. Visitors can be your friends, parents, siblings, or—in my case—your kids. One thing about remotes is we are proud of what we are doing. We take great pride knowing we are looking at life differently and becoming part of a revolution. Through our inspiration that comes from working and living around the world comes motivation—motivation to share. We want to share a glimpse of what it's like to live this life. We want to show off the excitement and introduce our guests to the friends we have made and the places we have lived.

Your company can feed such a desire to share—and secure an immediate POD—by providing your remotes with companion passes. Simply put, after specific goals or targets are met, your standout remote employees can qualify for companion passes—that is, airline tickets for loved ones or friends to visit the remotes in the countries where they're currently living and working. The concept is simple and affordable, and the value add for the remote is phenomenal.

In my experience, I found most remotes don't stray from their standard work routines when they have visitors. However, that's not always the case. The companion pass can also be used as an excursion invitation of sorts. Such a reward provides the hardworking remote the ability to recharge, a necessity when working from different time zones and navigating the wear and tear that accompanies the demands of living abroad.

The top question I get when others want to know about my experience is, "Where is your most favorite place that you've lived?" I explain to them that it's impossible for me to answer such a broad question. When you work and live in so many places, you end up falling in love with them for different reasons. You will almost always find something about a city that is your favorite part that ranks at the top of a particular category. For instance, you might have enjoyed the best food in Valencia, Spain, met a new friend in Lisbon, Portugal, had a fantastic roommate in London, or—in my case—had your son come visit you in North Africa!

My son, Jake, was twenty-three years old when he flew halfway around the world to stay with me in Morocco. I was working in the capital city of Rabat, a city with a population of just over six hundred thousand. Rabat is on the Atlantic Ocean and sits at the mouth of the Bou Regreg River. Morocco has two official languages: modern standard Arabic and Amazigh. French serves as the second language. When I told my kids I was going to be living around the world, I invited each of them to pick a country and city of their choice. Then I offered them to come and experience their visit through the eyes of a remote.

Jake immediately wanted to come to Prague, which, in hindsight, would have been a fabulous place to host my son. However, Prague was my first new home, and I was cautiously aware that I was not sure how this lifestyle was going to kick off. I encouraged him to select another country. He chose Morocco.

Without doing a lot of research in advance, Jake and I both had different expectations of what we would be getting into during our time in Africa. Those expectations surrounded the language, the distance from the United States, and, for my son, I think there was also some initial culture shock.

Jake's visit with me came at the perfect time. I had been gone for six months, I missed my kids, and I knew this visit was just as good for me as it was for him.

COMETS, CAMELS, AND FEAR...OH MY!

I wanted to do something special when Jake came to visit. I had already been living in Rabat for a couple of weeks prior to his arrival and had wished he had come to visit the month before when I was living in Lisbon, a top city on my list. However, I was committed to making the best of it—and we did!

Three days after Jake arrived in Casablanca, he and I were hailing a cab to get us to the train station for a four-hour-and-fifty-three-minute train ride to Marrakesh where we would treat ourselves to a short night's sleep, shisha, cold beers, and a couple of shots of Moroccan rum before beginning our trek.

Danny, one of my favorite people I lived with for a year,

is from Nijmegen, the Netherlands. An aggressive entrepreneur by day and fun-loving DJ by night, he—along with Stephan—had taken the lead on planning a private five-day road rally-style event that would take myself, ten remotes, and our guide into the world's largest, hottest desert—the Sahara. In Arabic, the Sahara is known as "The Greatest Desert" (الصحراء الكبرى) and has an area of 9,200,000 square kilometers—comparable to the size of China or the contiguous United States.

No insurance. No guardrails. No expectations. Stu, Danny, and Stephan had prior driving experience in adventure landscapes, and our professional guide, Marco, knew the land—I guess as much as you *can* know the land. We *all* had a thirst for adventure and took turns driving one of three brand-new trucks first through the streets of Marrakesh and then for hours and hours of winding, tire-carved dirt roads. The wind and dust whipping through the hefty truck's interior, combined with the classic rock blaring through the speakers, left us amped with excitement.

To get to the Sahara, though, we had to first drive through small, dilapidated villages in rural North Africa like Zerkten, Tazart, Ouarzazate, Tata, M'Hamid El Ghizlane, and finally Aznaguen. As we entered Aznaguen at about three to five miles per hour, something bright came into my peripheral vision. Then, I saw her: first, one young girl, about eight years old, running toward our slow-moving truck. Her smile was wide, and her right hand was waving like a windmill at full speed. Then, three more young girls appeared from clay huts with thatched roofs and no doors, their dresses were colorful and their smiles wide. Now, all four of them were running and hollering at the top of their lungs in what sounded almost like a chant. Between the roll of the tires and the engines in the trucks, I could not make out a word they were saying, although it wouldn't have helped much if I could have heard—I don't know a word of Arabic.

The day before, the twelve of us were staying in a four-star hotel, eating cheeseburgers, smoking shisha, and sipping rum. Now we were in a different place seeing people with different needs and expectations just hours outside Marrakesh. As we waved back at the young girls, I turned to Marco and asked what they were chanting. He looked over the top of his sunglasses and said, they are asking for "Pencils, candy, coins." It's a memory seared into my mind; the smile on my face from their excitement was gone. That moment could not have been more real. I turned to Jake on my left and said, "I will come back here again, and I promise you, I will bring boxes of pencils, handfuls of candy, and pockets full of coins."

The Sahara Desert isn't all sand dunes, hot sun, camels,

and drought—that's part of it, of course, but it's truly massive. Much of the area is rocky high desert, with cliffs, peaks, dirt, and gravel. It was there that I learned Jeremey, Jake, Chase, and Brian fell into one of three driving categories: hadn't driven a stick shift in more than ten years, learned to drive a stick shift the week before, or had never driven a stick shift. The reason why I know this is true is because three of these four macho men were in the truck with me while we were traversing the scariest stretch of road I have ever been on—steep climbs, loose rocks, gravel, and sheer half-mile cliffs on both sides of the road. When we made it to the top, we pulled over and enthusiastically manned up, hugged one another, and celebrated with a round of high fives.

Our overnight destination was even more surreal than the drive to get there. It was like we were in a movie, surrounded by pure, driven sand dunes as high as seven-story buildings. Once camp was set, we were ready to stretch our legs. Marco had brought along several what I would call snowboards—or, at least what I *knew* as a snowboard. All of us set out to take on the dunes. That afternoon, I captured my favorite picture of the more than sixteen thousand I had taken in 365 days. I was standing at the bottom of a forty- or fifty-meter high dune. At the top were my buddies Chase and Brian, with my son, Jake, all on snowboards. Their faces aren't visible, but you can see their bodies in silhouette fashion. There, behind the sun, they're holding snowboards above their heads like champions on the Olympic pedestal.

I'll never forget them sand-boarding down the dune to basecamp, another throwing a rope down and pulling the board back up, then walking around the back of the dune and doing it again. Remote life and adventure, encapsulated. It's the kind of inspiration that never leaves you.

During our first night in the desert, I learned from one of my friends, Stephan, that we would soon be witnessing the biggest meteor shower in seventy-five years. Not surprisingly, it turns out the scientist from Amsterdam was right. Two hours later, in the middle of the Sahara Desert with the dunes in the background, the sky was lit with meteors and shooting stars. It was cataclysmically bright, so much so that it looked like daylight across the expansive dunes. I felt so alive, like the air around me was charged. Stephan and I have recounted many times how that night was one of our most favorite events from the entire year. It all fell into place—the dunes, the night sky, the pulse of adrenaline, and the electricity of the adventure. And getting to share all of it with my son? The experience was the definition of work for reward.

WHAT ABOUT WORK?

Being part of the location-independent workforce isn't an excuse to travel and party in place of doing *actual* work. Quite the opposite. We worked our asses off. When you hire the right remote, they'll do the same for you.

Because it's such a competitive space, the average remote is far above the average, standard employee. That's true in terms of practical skills, but even more so in terms of their ability to be self-starters. They know they need to be focused, ambitious, and obsessed with giving a good name to remote workers, because if they don't, their company (and others) won't buy in to keeping them for the long term.

I understand that upper management is often fearful of hiring remote workers. They wonder what their location-independent staff members are doing all day. It's also reasonable that they worry about being out of touch and unable to control a process.

Here's the common denominator: Working remotely doesn't *create* a good employee. It doesn't take a below-average cubicle worker and make him or her great. It's not transformative. If remotes treat the opportunity like a vacation, their experience will last about as long as a vacation.

What the model *is*, however, is a talent reserve. It's an acquisition model for finding and keeping great talent, because great people do their best work when inspired. For myself and the top-performing remotes I've met, our metrics for productivity—sales conversions, creativity, and more—were all higher than those of our cubicle cohorts.

A perfect example of an inspired, top-performing remote is Alicia (Lish). I think the term *best friend* is too overused today. It's easy to text "my BF," "my BFF," or overuse it in an endearing way with dozens of friends. The dictionary, however, defines the term very simply—it's a person's closest friend. When I use the definition straight out of the dictionary, there is no question in my mind or heart that Lish was my closest friend the last eight months of living and working around the world.

Lish is a triple threat: attractive, fun, and smart. At five foot six, her blond hair and ocean-blue eyes turned heads from passersby in every country we lived. I used to tease her by telling her I now know what it's like to hang out with a celebrity. It didn't matter if we were living in Europe or South America, she stood out. Lish, though, was genuinely oblivious to the head turning and stares from the passersby, and that's no surprise. She is the least self-promoting, most awkwardly introverted friend I have ever had.

I had known Lish for four months before she disclosed in an offhand conversation that she had her master's degree in interdisciplinary social sciences and secondary education. It was not until we moved to South America 2 months later that I found out Lish spoke fluent Spanish. She learned Spanish while living in Guatemala and teaxching at an orphanage for for several years after college. When you listen to Lish talk about her past you can't help but think of a Reese Weatherspoon movie. I would learn over the next eight months the complex layers that made this thirty-two-year-old the insanely successful project manager at her Washington, DC-based commercial real estate firm.

I hope by now you are starting to see the consistencies in the profiles of my location-independent friends—the diversity, the strength, the loyalty, the inspiration, the personality, and the overall talent.

Even further, I hope as you read, you see this is all a numbers game. I could have included thirty profiles and stories of other remotes or locals I now know and call friends. I would work with all of them if there were ever enough time in a day, but I am one man who could only be in one place at a time.

You, though? You can do more.

WHAT IF?

- What if your only responsibility was to identify amazing talent around the world?
- What if you are a forward-thinking CEO of a company with a thousand employees and had resources?
- What if you are an HR executive with three hiring managers who wanted to be location-independent professionals?
- What if your next raise, bonus, or promotion was based on your winning the talent war?
- What if your job depended on your winning the talent war?

Don't we all want to meet, hire, and retain the Justins, Dhivyas, Tylers, Ee Yeens, and Lishes of the world? Winning the talent war means going to battle with your competitors. It means beating them at their own game. I would happily go to battle with the people I've written about in this book—and I'd win every time.

FINDING INSPIRATION WHEREVER YOU GO

You can find inspiration wherever you go—even if you go it alone. Ee Yeen taught me that. Ee Yeen is smart, hardworking, quiet, funny, strong, determined, and bossy. In fact, writing *bossy* still makes me laugh. Ee Yeen isn't *conventionally* bossy, but when you need to get something done, she's going to tell you in a giddy-up style. Sometimes, it was which train to get on, directing me about a deadline on an upcoming podcast, or, on rare occasions, it was being very specific on which Scotch whisky to order from the bartender. I quickly discovered Ee Yeen to be a very private, personal woman. Few got to know her well, but those of us who did appreciated her, confided in her, and knew thet we could depend on her.

At thirty-four years old, Ee Yeen was born as the oldest of three siblings in Ipoh, the capital city of the Malaysian state of Perak. The third largest city in Malaysia by population, Ipoh is home to more than seven hundred thousand. Very quickly after meeting Ee Yeen, it became obvious why this woman was selected from almost seventy thousand applicants to be part of our remote tribe. She speaks three languages, studied finance at the University of Technology Sydney in Australia, and worked in the corporate travel department at one of the world's largest *Fortune* 100 companies.

Throughout the book, I've described embedded remotes, gig/garage teams, and now Ee Yeen, a solo remote. Her story is an important one.

Ee Yeen, Lish, and I were sitting on the terrace at the Ambar restaurant, yards away from the amazing Danube

River, which is the second largest river in Europe. I had no idea over the next several months that the 1,777-mile-long river would intersect my journey three more times when I visited Bratislava, Vienna, and Budapest. I looked out on the water, knowing we were just days away from our travel weekend that would relocate us to London. The UK was not on our original itinerary. But because of the recent instability in Istanbul, Turkey and U.S. travel warnings we were rerouted to London.

The indescribable sunset and the therapeutic flow of the Danube made our cocktails, homemade kulen (flavored sausage made with minced pork), and Zlatarski cheese (soft white brined cheese from cow's milk) taste even better. I could tell from the moment I sat down with the girls that a second shoe would drop at dinner.

Before the main course was delivered, the always-steadfast and centered Ee Yeen was stumbling on her words. Then, without hesitation, she said, "I'm leaving."

"We're all leaving," I said.

"No, I'm leaving Remote Year," she said.

I knew immediately Lish already knew, because Lish didn't even look her way, she focused her stare right on me.

"What's going on, Ee?" I asked.

She explained that the Remote Year model wasn't for her, and she admitted she had been struggling both personally and professionally with her decision. She was not getting the benefit of the inclusive Remote Year packaging. Admittedly, she liked to spend time on her own and travel on her own agenda—and she also believed she could do both less expensively if she left the program. I sat quietly and listened. I knew when Ee Yeen made up her mind, she didn't change it.

One of the best things about being a remote is the people you meet and the bond that builds so quickly and strongly. The opposite side, though, is there almost always comes a time when we have to do what's best for us as individuals, and that's what Ee Yeen was doing.

I didn't say much in response to Ee Yeen's decision. Quietly, I nodded my head, recognizing for the first time but not the last time, I was going to have incredible friends all over the world when my year ended. I felt sad and elated all at the same time. The three of us had an incredible dinner. We closed the bar around 3:00 a.m., but only after exhausting the bartender of serving up every drop of Ee Yeen's favorite whisky.

Why is this story important to the book? You need to know

that amazing talent sometimes comes in the form of the solo artists like Ee Yeen, who are incredibly successful living and working around the world under their own sail.

TRAVEL CHANGES YOU: CEO EDITION

Once you have the foundation of a remote work situation—that is, you've done the research of where to live, how to fulfill your logistical work needs, and so on—you can let daily experiences invigorate you. You can land in a city and immediately have a high level of productivity wherever you are.

Many managers worry more about the length of time it took to complete a work task than the quality of the work itself. We want to see the progress of our employees—and, by extension, our companies—shaping daily. Many of us have type A personalities, but when we peel back the onion, what matters most is the end product.

When you have the right person working for you abroad, your needs align. You both know the end game is getting the job done and done right. Your remote employee will build his or her life around these needs, and that person will become very self-motivated and self-starting. Why? When something amazing is waiting outside your door, you work harder. When you hire good people and inspire them to do the work they love, then passion and productivity are commonplace.

It didn't take me long to get swept up into this new life of traveling the world and working remotely because the potential is limitless. That potential is rooted in the power of the gigonomy.

CHAPTER 5

BEHOLD: THE NEW GIGONOMY

Back in 2011, my business manager and I created a concept called "Team Genius" for our digital agency. I've always been fascinated by the interplay between intellectual intelligence and emotional intelligence and how balancing the two or more importantly marrying them together can often lead to massive innovation and quality gain—that is, the work of geniuses. The problem? High-IQ employees and high-EQ employees seldom seem to find their way to one another, even when they sit in the same office. Even as leaders, we tend to separate technical and creative workers as part of the work-flow process

When Yo!Dog still had an office, I began requiring that

each project be touched by at least two people—one of them had to be more left-brained and the other had to be more right-brained. The system felt unusual at first, but my team soon fell in love with it and started to build their own teams of genius without our having to tell them. It was as if for the first time, the creatives and the developers came together at the beginning of a project and worked through the entire process together. The quality of their output was proof enough for me: Team Genius stuck.

At first, Team Genius was limited to my small agency. As I decentralized and traveled, though, I continued to meet more and more talented people. I could visualize them working together and leveraging one another's strengths. My eyes grew a little wider every month as I realized Team Genius could go global, and it did—fitting squarely in the gigonomy where freelancers abroad would join forces to form impressive, high-performing teams with different skillsets.

THE GARAGE AGENCY, LOCAL GIG TEAM EXTRAORDINAIRE

I experienced two types of gig teams: first, self-organized groups of freelancers who perform all aspects of a project while living as remotes, and second, local teams—like the team of four from Belgrade, who still work with me today.

Both types of gig teams are powerful because their members realize they work well together and have diverse strengths. They market themselves as a one-stop shop of sorts. Some travel together, and others live in one place. My Belgrade team preferred the latter, quitting their individual office jobs to form what they deemed the "Garage Agency." Why? It's simple: being location independent meant they could *literally* work from anywhere, including their garage.

The Garage team I found in Belgrade consists of a front-end developer, a designer, a project manager, and Milan, the organizer—the Serbian city manager who first suggested I visit the majestic griffon vultures in that lush protected forest. The four bright young men all had traditional jobs but quit once they realized they could operate the Garage Agency on their own terms—and, even more importantly, that it could thrive. Together, they hack and reverse engineer our digital products, so my agency can get them to market quicker. I also use the team to push websites and apps to the edge, getting to the root of small issues before they become big, costly problems.

The setup is a win-win for both my company and this high-performing remote team. Because they're a true gig team, the Garage team completes entire projects without an ounce of outside help. As a CEO, hiring them means

I don't have the hassle and cost of finding, vetting, and managing handfuls of individual freelancers to do the same work. Plus, because they live in Serbia where the cost of living is significantly lower than it is in the States, it allows me to offer clients a better value and small businesses can noe afford to have more robust websites and access to technology that in the past they would not traditionally be able to afford.

The members of the Garage team are inspired, too. They can move from project to project and company to company, only taking the jobs they choose and are their own "boss," so they don't have to convince anyone to let them work from home—or, in this case, a garage. The team members are personally and professionally fulfilled, and they're working on projects all over the world. In fact, although the Garage team works with me regularly, I'm not their only client. They also work for a host of Eastern European companies. You can read more about their work at www. johnelston.com.

GIG TEAMS AND THE POWER OF SYNERGY

The Garage Agency is only one example of a gig team. There are many located all around the world, performing different tasks and marketing different skillsets. For this discussion, it's what they have *in common* that's most important: synergy. Uniquely, gig teams are autonomous as a collective, yet wholly dependent on one another for success. If one member underperforms, there isn't a CEO to assign a replacement. Throughout their work, then, is a solid undercurrent of accountability and performance that is coupled with—and I've seen it time and time again—the joy that comes with living an inspired life on your own terms. Much like location-independent remotes, members of gig teams often live activated lives. They build community with one another organically while living, working, and traveling together. Now, contrast this approach to the traditional community-building exercises that happen in companies today—organizing weekend-long corporate retreats, hosting fund raisers, or having happy hour every Wednesday. Compared to how a gig team operates, these attempts to bring people together are mere drops in the relationship bucket.

The success of gig teams around the world speaks to another larger point, too. The new paradigm of work is not solely about individual superstars. Yes, top talent counts—I still seek it today—but it's the talent shown in the output that matters, not the talent shown by one person in an interview. This point—this results-driven flexibility—becomes even more important when you consider that job descriptions are constantly changing.

It's simple. HR managers write job descriptions based on the company's needs *in that moment*. The person they hire, then, is expected to perform those tasks. But then what? What about when or if the candidate's talents fall *outside* that bulleted list? In the traditional hiring model, HR managers may never know if an employee is learning a new language, dabbling in 3-D animation, or taking art classes on the side. Gig teams, on the other hand, can likely perform every task on that same job description. But because they're only paid for project time, the company gets access to all their outside skills and the inspiration it brings into their work. The team is more likely to chime in with *balanced* creative input, too, because they're diverse professionally, and they're activated personally. It's the Team Genius concept in action.

THE VALUE OF TEAMS ABROAD

By hiring people abroad—whether solo remotes or gig teams—companies can get the same quality work—or better—for a fraction of the price. Why? I mentioned that the cost of living is lower in most places, for starters, but it's also largely true that working remotely is, in a way, *part of the payment* for someone with boots on the ground. Experiences are a big chunk of the compensation package. The point of the location-independent lifestyle, especially when there's travel involved, is to meet your needs *financially*—which is often easier because there's no astronomical rent and so on—and *personally*. It's that balance that makes remote workers the largest source of untapped talent.

Let me say that again, in case you missed it. Remote workers are the largest source of untapped talent. Period. Why? They live and work inspired. They pack some serious problem-solving skills. They're self-motivated. They work quickly. They connect with and often harness the talents of other remotes. Their geographical unavailability makes them unattractive to many companies, which means they have to perform *higher* at a *lower* cost to win projects.

Now, does that mean that becoming a remote will make a person an incredible employee? Absolutely not. Just like in hiring for traditional, location-dependent roles, it's exceptionally important for employers to be selective when hiring remotes to embed or gig teams to use on a project-by-project basis. What leveraging location independence and the power of the gigonomy *can* do, however, is take already great employees and make them spectacular.

CHAPTER 6

THE ULTIMATE POD

Location independence supports many positive qualities in the right candidates. They are often more well-rounded, creative, connected, and in touch with themselves and the work they do. In short? They're fired up personally and professionally. I'm fired up just thinking about more companies leveraging this untapped talent pool to move their businesses forward in a world that's increasingly competitive. How? There are several ways you or your company can join the Remote Revolution.

OPTION 1: EMBED A REMOTE

The option of hiring an embedded remote is near to my

heart because, frankly, that's what I am. I'm permanently location independent in my position as CEO of Yo!Dog. An embedded remote, though, doesn't have to be the CEO of a company. That person doesn't even have to be in HR. Instead, they can be any current or prospective employee who is passionate about travel and remote work. They are inspired by living abroad and can identify amazing talent around the world. Your company and the selected employee would do due diligence beforehand, planning to gather data along the way to assist your organization in evaluating the effectiveness of the program. It's a simple way to ease into remote work with one or two people—and ensure it is indeed the right path for the business—before any overarching policies are changed.

Other travel-minded employees will likely ask how they could come to be embedded, too. In this instance, the fortune of the embedded remote can be used as healthy motivation for those still in the office. If the company's initial launch of an embedded remote is a success, decision makers could put an incentive system in place to inspire office staff to work harder to earn a shot at becoming the next embedded remote.

For the company itself, the risk is small, but the payoff is substantial. The embedded remote benefits, of course, because they get to work while traveling, living fully activated and reveling in new experiences found far outside a cubicle.

OPTION 2: HIRE A GIG TEAM

Hiring a local gig team with a proven track record is the quickest way to leverage the Team Genius approach. Companies that do so will claim some of the best talent in the world, even while on a limited time schedule and budget. If your company already has one or several embedded remotes, finding a reputable gig team—perhaps even assembling one from fellow gigonomists—might happen organically. If there is no embedded remote to do the vetting, though, finding the *right* gig team will be critical to the success of the investment.

The right gig team, regardless of industry, will prioritize and be able to provide examples that speak to the quality of their output, responsiveness of their service, and speed of their work. It's also important to view the hiring of a gig team as simply that—a *gig*. Projects have beginnings and endings, diminishing the overall risk for the company and inspiring the gig team to work harder and faster. All companies already have synergistic teams that utilize teamwork, soft-touch skills, and high-touch skills. That's nothing new. Gig teams are different, though, in that they're one-stop shops that can give your company access to elite talent for short bursts of time, all without geographical restrictions or long-term costs.

OPTION 3: THE SOLO ARTISTS

Today, there are more location-independent solo artists (like Ee Yeen) than ever. In fact, I believe it is the fastest growing segment of location-independent professionals. Hiring solo artists unquestionably presents the lowest resource risk option to your business. Think of them as freelance or contract workers who will also be a great gateway to other remotes, as the internal network is ever strong.

OPTION 4: COUPLES / PARTNERS

I didn't spend much time on the couples option in the pages of this book, but it cannot be overlooked. They say things come better in twos, and I witnessed this firsthand by observing long-term relationship couples living and working around the world as a team. I was envious of the couples I worked with and got to know who had their own Team Genius—couples like Stephan and Liesbeth, both scientists from Amsterdam.

Stephan and Liesbeth are an incredible example of how to successfully take a relationship abroad. This power couple works together and interdependently of each other. Sometimes, they choose to live together in the same apartment, and other times, they stay independently of each other, opting instead to reside with friends. Only about 8 percent of our entire group at Remote Year fit into this category, but I know this segment of remote life has huge potential.

PEOPLE MAKE THE DIFFERENCE

Throughout this book, I've covered a host of substantial benefits your company can enjoy if you begin actively taking steps to embrace the Remote Revolution. At the core of each step, however, are the people.

As a CEO, one of the unexpected benefits of decentralization was an immediate increase in my own morale as well as my team's morale. The remotes I've hired are always more eager and entrepreneurial employees. They take more initiative and ownership, frequently looking for ways to go beyond the job description.

Do you remember the first time you were allowed to sit at the adult table at Thanksgiving? Remote employees feel like they have graduated to the professional adult table. They finally feel trusted, empowered, and free—a combination that unleashes innovation and loyalty in everything they do.

I've learned that employees are appreciative and display a higher level of dedication to their work when you trust them with the responsibility of working remotly. In fact, remote workers have even directly referred me to other qualified remote talent without being prompted—something that rarely happened organically in my decades of working in teams and corporate environments. Being location independent opens logistical doors, and builds a community of support within this growing pool of talent. My colleagues, employees, and location independent friends are excited about being a part of a revolution and they want to see it succeed.

Soon after I announced Yo!Dog was going all in on location-independent work, Andrew—the first approved Yo!Dog remote employee who later started the standing ovation when I announced I had decentralized the office—came to me with a friend of his who could help with our new production company. It was as if suddenly he no longer felt like he was on the *outside* of the business—ironic, because we no longer had an office building so he felt like anyone could be part of our team.

Bottom line: instead of posting jobs online and sifting through hundreds of applications based on geography, as a savvy company, you should consider hiring or embedding remote employees. The upside? Location-independent work is an easier sell to a better pool of talent. That's how you get to a POD. That's how you get genius work going.

COMING FULL CIRCLE

Now that my stint at Remote Year is complete, it's clearer to me than ever that location-independent work isn't something that *ends*. In fact, it's rooted in beginnings— the beginning of new experiences, new partnerships, and new opportunities. Did I start with this love and respect for remotes, both being one and hiring them for my business?

Hell no.

I started as a kid wearing a suit and tie, carrying a lunch box disguised as a briefcase. Then, I became the most dedicated paperboy in Ontario, California. Next, I worked as a bellman turned hotel executive turned start-up CEO.

And now? Less than one year ago, I was trekking to the Bosnian border to explore the habitat of the majestic griffon vulture. I was watching a meteor shower in the Sahara, my son by my side. I was meeting new people in every city, of the 8 countries I lived in, learning about and connecting with them *like it was my job*. Because, in a way, it was. I took all those experiences back into my professional endeavors, doing the most inspired work of my life and hiring the most talented people I'd ever met.

I'm still the same entrepreneur and opportunity-focused leader I've always been. This time, however, I focus on working for reward—the reward of experiences. I look at life differently. On that unique intersection where life and work collide, I see the largest source of untapped talent out there.

In a way, my life has had a Benjamin Button-like trajectory. I'm a millennial in a baby boomer's body. I became an adult when I was young. I had lots of responsibility at a young age, much of which required sacrifice. I didn't go to bars because I was running a bar. I didn't go out to restaurants because I was a maître d' and learning to cook. I didn't travel much because I was takng care of travelers When I was twenty, I worked and focused like a forty-year-old. This journey into the Future of Work has aligned me perfectly for the next season of my life. Now, I couldn't imagine living or working any other way.

My unique position allows me to engage with and shape the Future of Work for my children's generation. I'm not just seeing the revolution; I'm participating in it. I've traded my butcher-papered "briefcase" for twenty-three kilos of luggage. Now, I know I don't need a multi-million-dollar office building; I just need a quality daypack, a passport, and a smartphone, good wifi, and the vision to keep one foot in the future. As I write the last few pages of this book I am living and working in yet another country. I again feeling inspired and motivated. My 24 year old son is making lunch in the kitchen my Dog Kevin is here getting his normal 16 hour a day sleep and I am excited to share and teach my son who has committed to living and working as a location independent professional with me for the next six months.

GET OUT THERE!

For many, this book is probably an introduction to the idea of embedded remotes, gig teams, and other location-independent professionals circulating within the gigonomy. I understand the revolution feels fresh, but as with anything new and exciting, it's also clear there's a hint of adrenaline running through the veins of the Future of Work. That future, by the way, is now. With such a change comes great opportunity. How can you get involved?

Take baby steps and help define the location-independent professional, bringing that individual to your company. Reserve some of your budget for embedded remotes or gig teams. Sell the idea of remote work to your boss and offer to be the embedded remote. Share this book with possibility-focused colleagues and friends. Reach out to me at linkedin.com/in/johnelston or visit www.johnelston.com to learn more about my journey and how your company can leverage location-independent workers to get ahead. It's up to you to challenge the norm—work for reward and create your own reality.

EPILOGUE

I believe in the remote workforce, and I believe they have the power to change your company for the better. They're so much more than what can be described with worn-out clichés and trite statements. This group is bold, enlightened, and not afraid to get their hands and feet dirty. They reject cynicism and opt instead for possibility and hope, looking for opportunities that spark positive change for themselves, their companies, and the world.

Remotes think both linearly and circuitously. They're OK with moving goalposts—in fact, they *love* moving goalposts—because they find it exciting to be ever innovating on the cusp of a game that's always changing. Collectively, they thrive on being challenged and rise to the occasion with an arsenal of tools.

All too often in business, I see people having the wrong conversations because they have so many filters—filters that place constraints and limit thinking. I hate the term *outside the box*, but it's appropriate here because that's the area from which most businesses function: inside a box full of perceived and real barriers, the perceived ones often are as firmly implanted as the real ones.

Remotes cut through that noise because they have a much broader understanding of life; they aren't trapped by localized sentiment. A global view puts things into perspective.

I hope my book helps build a bridge and shortens the gap between the remote workforce for the large and small businesses around the world. Ultimately, my wish is that the truths and stories shared in this book will expose *your own* inner sense of adventure.

Ask yourself this question: "Would you rather hire an employee who could negotiate the mall parking lot with ease, or would you rather hire the *remote* who just managed to get from Nairobi to Paris during an airline strike *and* a coup while still meeting deadlines?" I know whom I'd choose.

WHAT'S NEXT?

On October 14, 2012, daredevil Felix Baumgartner ascended to the "edge of space" in a pressurized capsule suspended beneath a giant helium balloon before jumping out and free-falling for four minutes and nineteen seconds back to Earth from a height of 129,000 feet—all for the Red Bull Stratos project.

While companies don't want to necessarily jump from space themselves, they want to be known as the company that funded and supported such innovation. Such fire. You want to say, "We hired Eddie, the badass who lives and works around the world and has made us better." The good news is that you can.

Sponsoring and acting on the Remote Revolution now *will* improve the strength of your team. It will give you a point of differentiation among your competitors, which, in turn, will allow you to jump from space while sitting behind the comfort of your desk. It will give your company the fuel—the vision, understanding, clarity, and agility that is VUCA Prime—to thrive in a competitive marketplace full of shifting goalposts. The rules are already changing. You can watch from the sidelines, or you can gain a competitive advantage by leveraging a team of talented, inspired remotes who look at life differently.

The Future of Work is now. Join us.

ACKNOWLEDGMENTS

LIFELINES

- John Pla for too many things to write.
- PeggySue O'Rourke, my guardian angel.
- Colleen Montini for keeping her eye on the ball.
- Toni Jacaruso for early support and being in the room on day one.
- Rodney Pierini for convincing me I had a year to give.
- Paula Gil for being the Brazilian Portuguese Ninja.
- Tucker Max for allowing me to be number two behind him.
- Nalini Galbaransingh for your early encouragement and marketing push at the finish line

MY ROOMIES

- Tyler Duzan—Prague
- Chase Hitchens—Belgrade
- Alex Pomeranets—London, Medellín
- Matt Rudnitsky—Valencia
- Stu Parker—Lisbon
- Chris Pelican—Rabat, Lima
- Liesbeth Smit—Lima
- Dhivyakrishnan Radhakrishnan—Bogotá, Medellín
- Alicia Massey—Mexico City, Bogotá, Medellín
- Julimir Tovar—Buenos Aires, Medellín

R.Y.

For your sacrifices and amazing experiences:

- Jenna Winn
- Aline Yatema
- Tyler Toboada
- Milan Krêadinac
- Darien Tribe

REMOTE REVOLUTION TEAM

- Mark Chait, Book Developer, for the strategy and recommendations.
- Kathleen Pedersen, Publisher, for making the tough decisions.
- Jessica Burdg, Editor, for your patience, dedication, and continuous support.

ABOUT THE AUTHOR

JOHN ELSTON'S career started in the hospitality sector, where he worked his way up from bellman to partner in one of the country's largest hotel companies. He continued to operate hotels and resorts around the world until 2010, when he launched his start-up, a successful digital marketing agency. After several years of success, he decided to take his business on the road and pursue the future of work, spending fifteen months living and working around the world. John's passion, energy, and experiences working remotely on five continents along with his decades of executing successful business strategies make him a sought-after speaker and expert on harnessing the power of the location-independent workforce. He is a deeply passionate champion of the remote movement.